INFORMAL PUBLIC TRANSPORT IN PRACTICE

Informal Public Transport in Practice

Matatu Entrepreneurship

MELECKIDZEDECK KHAYESI
Transport Researcher, Geneva, Switzerland

FREDRICK MUYIA NAFUKHO
Texas A&M University, USA

JOYCE KEMUMA
Dalarna University, Sweden

ASHGATE

Published by
Ashgate Publishing Limited
Wey Court East
Union Road
Farnham
Surrey, GU9 7PT
England

Ashgate Publishing Company
110 Cherry Street
Suite 3-1
Burlington, VT 05401-3818
USA

www.ashgate.com

British Library Cataloguing in Publication Data
A catalogue record for this book is available from the British Library

The Library of Congress has cataloged the printed edition as follows:
Khayesi, Meleckidzedeck.
Informal public transport in practice : matatu entrepreneurship / by Meleckidzedeck Khayesi, Fredrick Muyia Nafukho and Joyce Kemuma.
 pages cm – (Transport and society)
 Includes bibliographical references and index.
 ISBN 978-1-4094-4692-7 (hardback) – ISBN 978-1-4094-4693-4 (ebook) – ISBN 978-1-4724-0623-1 (epub) 1. Local transit–Kenya. 2. Paratransit services–Kenya. 3. Bus lines–Kenya. 4. Urban transportation–Kenya. I. Nafukho, Fredrick Muyia. II. Kemuma, Joyce. III. Title. IV. Series: Transport and society.
 HE311.K4K43 2015
 388–dc23

2015006541

ISBN 9781409446927 (hbk)
ISBN 9781409446934 (ebk – PDF)
ISBN 9781472406231 (ebk – ePUB)

Printed in the United Kingdom by Henry Ling Limited, at the Dorset Press, Dorchester, DT1 1HD

Contents

List of Figures, Tables and Boxes

Figures

Tables

Boxes

Foreword

Dorothy McCormick

'Matatu' and 'Entrepreneurship' are words that rarely appear on the same page, let alone in a book title. Yet this accessible and creative book has married them in a way that begs readers to reflect on a public transport reality that Kenyans and other Africans often dismiss as an unavoidable nuisance. In contrast to the common description of the matatu industry as chaotic, reckless, and rude, this book argues that it is a 'self-organising industry ... situated in a dynamic transport, socio-economic, and political environment in Kenya' (see page 8).

The collaboration of three authors with deep Kenyan roots – Meleckidzedeck Khayesi, Fredrick Muyia Nafukho, and Joyce Kemuma – has produced a serious analysis that draws on their respective strengths in transport and road safety, educational administration, and learning and knowledge acquisition. The authors, synthesizing extensive evidence on the lived experience of the matatu industry, show that the matatu has not only carved out a business niche in Kenya, but has also created its own practical business logic. Out of this has emerged a broad network of individuals, groups, and organisations which the authors depict as a matatu tree with branches extending in many directions and roots sunk into Kenya's political economy (Figure 3.1). While the downside of the matatu industry cannot be denied, understanding its roots, branches and learning processes can help stakeholders to take it to a higher level without destroying its creativity and flexibility.

A few years ago, when framing some new research, colleagues and I realised that most transport experts fail to recognise that in Kenya and much of Africa, those small, loud, sometimes abusive vehicles are actually business enterprises. As researchers in the field of enterprise and development, we thought that we had a contribution to make to the prevailing discourse. The resulting research has been revealing and, I believe, useful in re-conceptualising the matatu industry. This book takes that re-conceptualisation and its implications several steps forward. It allows the matatu to speak for itself, saying confidently, 'My name is matatu' (see page 3). It digs into the soil in which the matatu was born and continues to grow in urban and rural Kenya including M-Pesa, the harambee movement, greenbelt movement, Iko toilet project, adopt-a-light project, and the Marakwet-Keiyo traditional irrigation system. It analyses the industry in itself rather than as a second cousin to the Western variants of formal transport, and it rightly recognises the matatu as an entrepreneurial venture. From their grounding in these realities, the authors challenge policy makers and strategic thinkers to draw lessons from the matatu industry that can be used to facilitate the development of better public transport services for the people of Kenya.

I congratulate the authors, Melecki, Fred, and Joyce. You have produced a book that many will want to read and that, I believe, is destined to become a classic in the field.

Preface

'What really is the matatu industry?' This is a question that has occupied the minds of several researchers from different disciplines for several years. While some researchers and practitioners see the matatu entrepreneurship as beneficial to society, others see it as an embodiment of all that is wrong in Kenya. The three of us have also struggled with understanding the matatu industry. For example, Khayesi wondered whether to call the matatu structure an empire of chaos in a paper published in 2002. Again, in 2002, Kemuma, Murunga and Khayesi struggled with whether to look at the youth working in the matatu industry as a notorious workforce. While these scholars have looked at different aspects of the matatu industry and come out emphasizing one aspect or the other, each adding to our understanding of the industry, our contribution with this book is in examining the matatu industry as a multi-layered entrepreneurial undertaking with a sophisticated and expanding trajectory embedded within the dynamic Kenyan historical, political, economic and social makeup.

Applying Bourdieu's (1990) concepts of *habitus*, field, social and economic capital, we realize that the matatu industry, whether seen as chaotic or as beneficial, is an organization with a logic of practice. Beneath the appearance of 'menace' and chaos, we have characterized the matatu entrepreneurship as a self-organizing sector within the wider fare-paying-transportation field with a well-established logic of practice and a matatu-specific-*habitus* of its own, that has grown over time. This logic of practice has been shaped by necessity in the broader historical and political economy of Kenya, leading to the emergence of the matatu *habitus* with its ways of seeing, doing and being. Subsequently, this *habitus* has led to the creation of a matatu culture with a system of rules and regulations, flexibility, adaptive capacity, organization, shared codes, learning experiences, business strategies and response to individual, organizational, community and national matatu-related issues. We show that this logic of practice has been and still is a fundamental principle that orients and governs matatu businesses. This logic of practice has therefore seen the matatu sector survive various political and economic regimes in Kenya in a Machiavellian way.

We conclude that matatu entrepreneurship is deeply embedded in everyday Kenyan life and is a formidable force that cannot easily be ignored in policy and practice. Given the way matatu entrepreneurship has transformed Kenyan society in many positive ways, it appears that this industry can become a learning organization that may offer lessons for informal and lifelong organizational learning in the 21st century and beyond. We believe that the industry will continue to participate in the economic and social wellbeing of Kenyan society at large.

Meleckidzedeck Khayesi, Fredrick Muyia Nafukho, Joyce Kemuma

Acknowledgements

We are grateful for the support we received from the following colleagues, friends and family members: Alfred Anangwe, Anna Nyaoro Mala, Peter Mala, Truphosa Kadasia, Jeanne-Marie Scott, Jane Nyakecho Khayesi, David Khayesi, Zipporah Shanyisa Khayesi, Painito Ajanga, Samuel Kimani, Felicia Arudo Yieke, Dorothy McCormick, Teri Reynolds, Rodney Asilla, Ruth Busolo, Patricia Alembi, Seth Ambei Stingo, Dolline Busolo, John Whitelegg, Margie Peden, Kenda Mutongi, Hellen Muyia Nafukho, Mary Muyia, Mercy Muyia, Nelly Muyia, Marianne Muyia, Emmanuel Muyia, Barbara Hinton, Michael F. Burnett, Carroll Graham, Yvonna Lincoln, Neslon W. Wawire, Glenda Musoba, Joseph Musoba, Misha Chakraborty and many others.

We are also grateful to the following institutions that provided scientific bases and support for our research on the matatu and other related topics over the years: Kenyatta University, Institute for Development Studies of the University of Nairobi, Organisation for Social Science Research in Eastern and Southern Africa, Moi University, University of Arkansas at Fayetteville, Louisiana State University, Baton Rouge, Louisiana, Texas A&M University (College Station, Texas), and Dalarna University in Sweden.

We thank the many scholars whose work on matatu, transport, political economy, entrepreneurship, environment and development we have drawn upon while preparing this book. We also thank change agents and initiatives whose efforts we have drawn upon to show examples of transformation and solutions to address social and ecological issues. We are indeed grateful to the Transport and Socicty Series Editor (Margaret Grieco) and staff (Katy Crossan, Carolyn Court and many others) of Ashgate Publishing Ltd for their unique developmental and collaborative approach to developing this book.

Chapter 1
'What is in a Name?'

Introduction

Movement of people, materials, freight and information is central to the functioning of society as well as its interaction (Urry 2007, Hoyle and Knowles 2001, Ogonda 1986, Abler et al. 1972). Movement is usually undertaken using different but complementary means of transport. These means include ropes, feet, pipelines, animals, bicycles, tricycles, motorcycles, motor vehicles, trains, boats, ships and airplanes. The increasing use of information and communication technology such as mobile phones and the Internet has not necessarily replaced the need for physical movement of people, freight and information. If anything, it has complemented and influenced movement and functioning of society, which include 'stimulation of more travel as new opportunities become available, substitution for travel as activities can now be carried out more remotely rather than by travel, and modification of travel, as the two elements combine to change the ways in which activities are carried out' (Banister 2005: 171). Any movement has an origin and a destination, as well as diverse characteristics that are of interest to researchers and planners. These characteristics include the following: trip purpose, trip length, types of route used, means of transport used, costs incurred, amount of time spent in travelling, amount of movement generated and direction of movement as well as externalities such as traffic congestion, transport-related pollution and road traffic crashes.

What means of transport does the public in different parts of the world use? While some societies and settings have subsidised public transport service provided by the state and/or public-private partnerships, others mainly rely on privately owned informal public transport service. It is this diversity in the way public transport service is organized and accessed in different parts of the world that adds depth, richness and challenging opportunities to sustainable and multimodal transport planning.

We tell the intriguing entrepreneurship story of the matatu service in this book. The matatu industry is a small-scale privately owned public transport business service in Kenya. This industry is actually the backbone of the public transport service in Kenya. We can look at it as the Kenyan version of paratransit or informal public transport service that is found in several developing and developed countries. The matatu is a household name in Kenya. The origin of the name is attributed to the original fare of 30 Kenyan cents charged to passengers in the 1950s and 1960s. Different types of vehicles are used for the matatu and paratransit service. Some are new and others are old; some carry a few passengers while others carry many passengers. The story is not just about the vehicle but of a system of entrepreneurship and a logic of practice or a way of doing things that has developed around this transport service. Though we use the specific experience of Kenya, we draw on examples of informal transport service from other countries around the world where appropriate, as well as from entrepreneurial initiatives in other sectors.

Kenya is located in East Africa. As at 2012, Kenya had a population of about 40.7 million people, occupying a land area of 581 309 km², and a gross domestic product per capita of Kshs. 39,607 ($455.51)[1] (Kenya National Bureau of Statistics 2014). A key word to describe Kenya is diversity. One notices diversity in climate, vegetation, economic activities and ethno-linguistic and religious groups. Agriculture is the major employer of most Kenyans. This chapter sets the stage for the book by introducing the matatu entrepreneurship phenomenon, explaining the research and planning context, as well as the need for the book.

The Matatu: Praised and Vilified

A well-known analogy in entrepreneurship research is that of likening the search for entrepreneur characteristics to the hunt for the heffalump. This analogy, attributed to Kilby (1971, 2003; Carland et al. 2001), goes as follows: the heffalump was a large and an important creature. Everyone reported having seen it, although each individual described it differently. Despite the absence of consensus on heffalump characteristics, no one would admit to not knowing what a heffalump was and everyone avowed that they could recognize one when they saw it. Applying this analogy to the matatu industry, it is evident from stories we have heard and evidence presented in studies that different people have encountered the matatu transport service in different ways, and use different words, perspectives and aspects to talk about the same phenomenon of the matatu entrepreneurship.

While some people focus on the vital transport service offered by this industry, others allude to a pervasive culture of chaos, violence and recklessness. To some, the matatu is a beneficial and necessary service, reflecting an entrepreneurial spirit and undertaking. To others, the matatu is a source of pain because they either lost their investment in the sector or a beloved one died when a matatu vehicle she was travelling in was involved in a road crash. Other people might have either been overcharged by matatu operators or were caught up in a conflict or violent incident involving the matatu industry. Even within the matatu service sector itself, there are several encounters and different contexts by which operators have come to know the matatu.

We also have personal experiences as researchers with regard to the meaning of matatu entrepreneurship. A reviewer of a research proposal submitted by Khayesi for funding in the 1990s almost dismissed it, arguing that it was not easy

---

1   This figure is calculated based on the current exchange rate of $1= Kshs. 86.950.

to interview matatu workers, which was the focus of the proposal; the reviewer felt that these workers were hooligans. The situation was partly saved by a fellow researcher who said that she was part of the Kapila et al. (1982) research assistant team that had managed to interview the 'hooligans'. She convincingly argued that they were not hooligans but rather workers eking out a living like any other professional. When Khayesi and his team of research assistants finally got to the field, they were indeed surprised to meet friendly matatu drivers and conductors, who offered the research team free rides and even meals. They discovered a complex network of relationships, transactions and depth of knowledge possessed by these workers, not just about the matatu sector but life in Kenya in general. The experience was an eye opener to a reality that the research team and the reviewer had not encountered first hand.

Another personal experience comes from Nafukho. He submitted a research proposal and received the first external grant in 1995 to examine performance of matatu drivers in relation to their involvement in road traffic crashes. In face-to-face discussions between all grantees and reviewers of proposals, a major issue that intrigued the reviewers of his proposal was the fact that there were very high numbers of road traffic crashes involving matatus and whenever a crash happened, almost all the people in the matatu vehicle, including the drivers, perished. The key question the reviewers asked was: 'Were the drivers committing suicide or were the working conditions among the matatu workers the main contributor to the high number of deaths from matatu-related crashes?' Like Khayesi's study (1997, 2001a), Nafukho (2001) established that matatu workers were eking out a living and not necessarily looking for spaces to commit suicide. He came to understand better the conditions under which matatu workers operated; no working contracts, cut-throat competition for passengers, profit maximization, long working hours and an overall demanding business environment. We have therefore decided not to try to describe the hunt for the matatu heffalump by ourselves but rather let the matatu speak for itself to give us insights into the diverse ways it is described and experienced by different people in Kenya and other countries in the world (see Box 1.1).

Box 1.1

Who am I?

My name is Matatu and I am called by different names in different countries of the world. While researchers are wondering whether to call me paratransit or informal public transport or mini-bus transport, and public officials are struggling with whether to classify me as a legal or an illegal business activity, the public is not short of names for me. While people in Lagos call me 'Kabu-Kabu', the honourable residents of Accra call me Tros Tros; in the Republic of Gambia, Tanka Tanka, and in Sierra Leone they call me Poda Poda. In Benin,

I am called Kia Kia. In the Democratic Republic of Congo I am known as Fula Fula; Mozambique, Chapa; Ugandans refer to me as Kamunye; South Africans just refer to me as taxi, while Tanzanians say I am Dala Dala. When I show up in India, I am called Polaamboo or Jeepneys; in Indonesia, Pete Pete; in Israel, Monit Sherut; in Yemen, Dabaab; in Japan, Noriaitakushī; in Macedonia, Kombe; in Mexico, Pesero or Combi; in Nepal, Micro; and in Russia, Marshrutka. Because I have been involved in road traffic crashes which alter the lives of many people, I am sometimes sadly referred to as a moving mortuary or a flying coffin.

I understand that there is someone in the United States of America who has a car number plate with my name written on it and an academic journal called Matatu Journal for African Culture and Society even exists in the land of the free and the home of the brave.

Figure 1.1   'Matatu' car registration plate, Kentucky, USA. Used with permission of owner Richard Bowen

I have also been reliably informed that someone in Sweden has a sticker on his car stating 'I love my matatu'. I also hear that my name has almost been submitted for consideration as the eighth wonder of the world. My cousin, Boda Boda, who uses bicycles and motorcycles to transport people and goods, informs me that I am the subject of scientific analysis and policy debates on how I can be transformed to become a better member of the society on wheels when the truth is that I have already transformed the society and I am even referred to as 'matatu culture', showing that I have created my values and style. I gather that some people have been awarded Masters and Doctorate degrees because of partly studying and analyzing my behaviour, travelling speed, size, number of people I carry and my overall performance. I suspect I am the subject of discussion in many households, offices, social meetings and many venues in Kenya as well as on Facebook, Twitter, Pinterest, WhatsApp, YouTube and other platforms on the Internet. When some people are unhappy with the way Kenyan leaders are behaving and ruling, they advise them not to rule the country as if it is a matatu. When some men have no confidence in their spouses, they refer to them by my name. In fact many songs have been composed in my name such 'Omukhasi/omusatsa matatu shakonanga munyumba ... ' (A wife/husband who is a matatu does not spend a night at home with her/his spouse). According to Kenyan traffic laws, also popularly known as Michuki laws, I am supposed to be painted in white colour with a broken yellow stripe around my body. However, I am painted in a variety of colours, and different names are written on my body, depending on the taste of the person or group that owns me. Some people choose to board me depending on my colour, name, and type of music, or WiFi services available. In fact the list of my names is so long that it can easily stretch across the entire Earth. Many people have wondered at my many names and they are never sure what or who the names are trying to appeal to. I am told a number of tourists who have explored Kenya maintain a whole diary filled with their travel experiences with me.

When it comes to describing the work I do, those who operate me prefer to send a warning to passengers: 'Hii Kazi ni Ngumu Tafadhali Lipa Bila Fujo' (This work is difficult, please pay without causing any trouble). In the towns of Nairobi, Mombasa, Nakuru, Kisumu and Eldoret, during rush hours and especially at the end of the month, I can be compared to the popular Kenyan diet, ugali (a white maize meal consumed by many Kenyans). Thus, I am to traffic what ugali is to dinner in Kenya. I am the staple food of Kenyan public transport service and the earnings got through my services are used to buy the flour for making ugali for many matatu workers and their families. I provide an important service to the education sector by transporting students and teachers to school on time. I also ensure efficient functioning of the economy by providing effective means of transport for people and goods.

I remember being seen as an illegal and pirate transport service when I started operating in Nairobi in the 1950s and grew further in the 1960s and 1970s. I have grown over time to become an integral component of the transport system and life in Kenya, not just in Nairobi but in the entire country. As far as I am concerned, I play an important role in the movement of goods and people in both urban and rural areas of Kenya. Before boda boda came of age, there were some rural and urban areas in Kenya where I was the only known public service vehicle that was reliable and people waited for me as if I was their lifeline. I provide shelter to several institutions and persons involved in transport service provision, repair work, ownership, regulation, importation, licensing, driver training and a network of businesses. When it comes to my efficiency, those who operate me on the road have perfected overloading me, disregarding traffic rules, poorly maintaining me, playing loud music, driving me carelessly, not maintaining transport standards and engaging in cut-throat competition. They also end up blaming me for all the mistakes they deliberately commit. In 2003, the Kenyan Government introduced Legal Notice No. 161 which aimed at ensuring that I offer an efficient, affordable and safe service to society but this notice has not been consistently implemented to achieve good results.

Depending on how those who operate me handle me during the day, I shall bring either happiness or sadness to my owner when I return home in the evening. In any case, I keep my owner awake until I am returned home in the evening or past midnight. Also, depending on the integrity of those who operate me, there is a happy relationship between my owner and those who operate me, especially when they honestly declare the day's collection to my owner. In some cases, I have witnessed dishonesty among those who operate me, especially when they lie to my owner that the day was so bad since there were no customers. I also feel bad when they deceitfully and shamelessly take all the day's collections instead of giving it to their employer, who is my owner. I have learnt over time that the dishonest workers hardly last and are always replaced. How I wish I could tell my story of the day to my owner when I return home. Unfortunately, nature does not allow me to tell the story in an overt way.

Source: Prepared by authors based on personal experiences and literature review (see for instance McCormick et al. 2013, Kinyanjui and Khayesi 2013, Schalekamp and Behrens 2013, Kamuhanda and Schmidt 2009, Graeff 2009, Cervero and Goloub 2007, Godard 2007, Valenzuela et al. 2005, Ngowi 2005, Rizzo 2002, Cervero 2000, de Soto 1989).

The contextual meanings presented in Box 1.1 show that the matatu form of transport service, as already indicated, belongs to the family of informal public or paratransit transport service that is found in many countries in Africa, Asia and South America. This service is an integral component of the public transport service and overall transport system in these countries (Mutongi 2014, Klopp et al. n.d, Cervero and Goloub 2009, Kamuhanda and Schmidt 2009, Ngowi 2005, Valenzuela et al. 2005, Cervero 2000, Midgley 1994, de Soto 1989). Paratransit service has been found appropriate for the communities it operates in, given deficiencies in scheduled bus or train services, low levels of income among the communities served, difficulties in physical terrain, short-distances of travel, low volume of goods carried, its flexibility and demand responsiveness (Mutongi 2014, Klopp et al. n.d., Behrens 2010). As is the case in Kenya, the informal and small-scale public transport sector in these countries is made up of a mix of both motorized and non-motorized modes, with variation in body design, passenger capacity and safety standards (Kwakye et al. 1997, Etherington and Simon 1996). Thus, when analyzing the matatu industry in Kenya, one needs to look at it broadly as a local manifestation of a global transport phenomenon and organization of society.

The central issue we are looking at with respect to matatu transport service and transport in general is movement of people, goods and information in space and time. This movement, which is part of human interaction, arises due to location and separation of human activities in time and space, and is conditioned by complementarity, intervening opportunity, transferability and utility as Ullman (1957) and Lowe and Moryadas (1975) have demonstrated in their conceptual models. Movement is an expression of the social organization of space and an attempt to achieve effective integration between specific locations of human activity. Movement could be considered as essentially a function of land use patterns, residential patterns, population densities, street geometry, location of work place, shopping precinct, health centre, and other traffic generation-attraction localities (Hoyle and Knowles 2001, Hilling 1996, Whitelegg 1987, Ogonda 1986, White and Senior 1983, Lowe and Moryadas 1975). There are several political, economic, social, technological and environmental factors that collectively influence the development and functioning of a transport system in any geographical setting (Hoyle and Knowles 2001). Transport networks, stock, flows and services, including the matatu industry in Kenya, are indeed part and parcel of the heritage and organization of any human society.

What This Book is About

One can rightfully question the added value of another book and a study on the matatu industry. After all, don't we know already everything about this sector? In any case, one may wonder: 'Why should researchers spend their valuable time studying what seems to be a chaotic sector instead of a productive activity?' We do not deny that the matatu industry is sometimes chaotic, violent and seems disorganized, infiltrated by cartels, criminals and corrupt practices. We examine these negative aspects in this book as well. What has struck us as we have looked below the surface is that contrary to the general perception of a chaotic matatu industry, there is a logic of practice in this industry that has evolved over a period of time. The matatu industry reveals how indigenous African entrepreneurship and capitalism straddles various economic, political and social systems. The growth path has witnessed not only opportunities but also problems and challenges, a number of which have continued to face the matatu industry up to now. This dynamism invites in-depth analysis and contextualization in order to understand how matatu entrepreneurship has been produced by the political economy of Kenya.

Drawing on over ten years of research and diverse sources of information, we situate the development of matatu entrepreneurship and its logic of practice in a historical, political and economic context. We combine theories, methods and insights to specifically examine how matatu entrepreneurs identified and mobilized resources and exploited the transport demand opportunity in order to play an important role in the day-to-day interaction and life of people in Kenya. We address the following specific questions:

a. What historical and contemporary political and economic factors have shaped the production of matatu entrepreneurship and its logic of practice?
b. How has matatu entrepreneurship in turn contributed to the formation and functioning of life in Kenya?
c. How has the matatu entrepreneurship performed?
d. What are the externalities associated with matatu entrepreneurship and how do they affect society?
e. What other entrepreneurial initiatives exist in Kenya?
f. What lessons does the matatu entrepreneurship offer to Kenya and other countries?

Results of the in-depth analysis conducted for this book lead us to contend that matatu entrepreneurship and its logic of practice have not only been produced and are deeply embedded in the historical and political economy of Kenya, but have also contributed to the creation of the Kenya society. We further contend that this industry has contributed to its own production by creating a logic of practice which it has utilized using various strategies to become an integral part of the transport system and political economy of Kenya. We therefore conclude that the matatu is not just a decontextualized, disembodied and lifeless piece of moving metal carrying people and goods but rather a self-organizing business. It has its logic of practice that is situated in a dynamic transport, socio-economic and political environment. The industry provides an essential transport service in both rural and urban areas of Kenya and several developing countries. There is a long-standing, mutual, beneficial and sometimes exploitative relationship between the matatu industry, the state and society. The matatu industry employs both confrontational and diplomatic strategies in its negotiation with the state. This complex relationship demonstrates the embeddedness of transport business or service in society. We invite the reader to explore the question: Are there lessons for society and all of us in this intriguing matatu entrepreneurship trajectory?

Summary

The key points in this chapter are as follows:

- The chapter has laid the background to the book, pointing out how the dynamics in the development of a self-organizing informal public transport service with its logic of practice invites an in-depth analysis and contextualization in order to understand how matatu entrepreneurship has been produced by the political economy of Kenya. For example, while the matatu industry is a beneficial and necessary service, reflecting an entrepreneurial spirit and undertaking to some people, to others the matatu is a pain and should be done away with.
- The chapter has shown the matatu form of public transport service to belong to the family of informal or paratransit public transport system that is found in many countries in Africa, Asia and South America and is an integral component of the transport system in these countries.

Chapter 2
Peeling off the Layers of the Matatu Entrepreneurship

Introduction

Our long involvement in research on the matatu industry and related themes has led us to a deeper reflection towards understanding the sector. Earlier on in our research, we grappled with how to view and describe the matatu industry. We even wondered or posed a question as to whether the matatu industry was an empire of chaos (Khayesi 2002) or considered the workers as a notorius workforce (Kemuma, Murunga and Khayesi 2002). Over time we came to understand several existing organizational layers, especially the way the sector operates as a system, organizes its labour and itself to respond to the demand for a public transport service. This understanding has led to a deeper analysis of the logic of practice of the matatu industry that is presented in this book. This chapter outlines the main conceptual frameworks we have utilized and describes the methods used to gather and analyse information for this book.

Which Lenses does One Use to Look at Matatu Entrepreneurship?

The process of exploring the appropriate conceptual frameworks and models to examine the matatu industry for this book has been like peeling off the layers of an onion in order to uncover its logic of practice. We learned the importance of allowing the matatu entrepreneurship phenomenon to reveal and speak for itself by looking at it from different perspectives and even permitting unexpected manifestations that do not fit into a chosen conceptual model to come through. We describe below how this process has led us to identify and construct our points of departure for this book.

The book takes four major points of departure from conventional transport research. The first point of departure is that it provides a nuanced analysis of the matatu public transport service and its embeddedness in society. This approach partly fills a gap in most of the conventional transport research, which concentrates on quantitative analysis of the transport network, travel behaviour and movement of goods (Vasconcellos 2001, Crang et al. 2013, Koglin and Rye 2014). While some progress has been made in transport research to utilize qualitative methods, most of the papers being published in journals still tend towards quantitative methods (Goety et al. 2009). If only the conventional quantitative approach was used in this book, it would have left out the intertwinement and complexity of matatu as a mode of transport within a historical, political and economic context. This book would consider mainly statistical modelling and leave out a deeper analysis of the life-world of transport, which partly involves looking at the contribution of transport to transactions in the everyday life of society. This omission in conventional transport discourse cannot continue given the fact that human beings are involved in different aspects of the transport industry, including operating vehicles that move goods and people in space and time.

There is a consensus in philosophy and practice of science that evidence does not refer to quantitative research only or that which is generated through the hypothetico-deductive rationalist mode of science but rather a combination of different perspectives and methods (Sandra et al. 2012, Eyben 2013). This view should continually remind transport researchers and other scientists about the need to pay sustained attention to political, social, economic and institutional factors in research and policy and not to advance only positivist transport research and planning models such as the four-stage transport-land use model, the land-use and transport integration model and the statistical modelling tradition as the main ways of knowing and studying transport topics and/or related issues in development (Vasconcellos 2001, Knoflacher 2009, Goety et al. 2009, Eyben 2013, Piketty 2014).

A review of transport studies in Kenya revealed a wide range of themes which have been examined, such as transport network growth and development, movement of goods and people, trip generation-attraction and the impact of transport (Khayesi and Ogonda 2001). These studies have been done at varying spatial scales; urban, rural, regional and national. Some have looked at specific transport modes, such as ports, road and railway, while others have concentrated on specific transport issues, such as household travel characteristics and the role of transport in economic development. The review further revealed that the road transport system had the largest number of publications, followed by other modes, such as air, water, non-motorized and rail in that order. In terms of levels of publication, post-graduate work dominated, accounting for over 30 per cent of all publications, with over 20 per cent of the work carried out at Masters degree level. Other publications are in the form of reports, conference and seminar papers, as well as undergraduate dissertations. Thus, a book on the matatu has to take into consideration the themes revealed in the review by Khayesi and Ogonda (2001). For instance, this book shows that the road infrastructure, petrol stations, insurance companies and socio-economic structures related to the matatu industry are part and parcel of the political economy and rhythm of life in Kenya. By adopting a deeper contextualization and applying social science theories and methods in a systematic analysis, this book highlights a number of issues that are rarely covered in the conventional quantitative discourse on transport entrepreneurship research. The book touches on politics, governance, human resource development, workers, employment creation, violence, gender and performance of the matatu industry.

The second point of departure is that the book provides a context-sensitive analysis of the matatu and informal transport in Kenya. Research on informal transport and other aspects of transport in developing countries often ends up comparing the situation in these countries with those prevailing in high-income countries. Although comparisons are necessary in research, the problem with the uncritical comparisons made in some transport research is the failure to highlight the relevance and strengths of what exists as a basis for policy formulation. We sometimes witness a transport discourse that concentrates on narrating what is missing in transport policy in developing countries as assessed against high-income countries rather than articulating the local creative processes and dynamics in responding to gaps in transport demand as revealed in the informal public transport modes such as the matatu, motorcycle and bicycle transport. This kind of situation has also been found in other areas of research such as urban and development studies. For example, Robinson (2002), McFarlane (2002) and Roy (2009) have observed that some scholars in urban studies tend to compare urbanization in developing countries with the global cities of the North, and miss a great deal of the processes that are important in the life of Southern cities. Chambers (1983, 2005) has shown how development research has tended to lack a deep engagement or immersion in the reality of communities. He has demonstrated that this disengaged research has led to superficial recommendations and shallow projects being implemented. He has challenged developement researchers and practictioners to reverse this tendency by listening and working with communities in a meaningful participatory way. In his critique of global development planning, Stigliz (2002) shows how decisions made and programmes implemented lack deep engagement with the reality on the ground.

We make an effort to go beyond the decontextualized and often one-sided discourse about the 'unruly and rowdy' informal public transport sector in developing countries by examining such key aspects as the organization of labour and the on-the-ground reality of an operation that involves multiple stakeholders. This book extends the growing effort by researchers such as Shorter and Onyancha (1997), Nafukho and Hinton (2003), Mutongi (2006, 2014), wa Mungai and Samper (2006), Cervero and Golub (2007), Graeff (2009), Rasmussen (2012), Schalekamp and Behrens (2013), McCormick et al. (2013) and Behrens et al. (2014), who examine the organizational structure, working conditions, performance improvement, and business dynamics of the matatu industry. We draw on these studies and even some of the relevant aspects in the one-sided studies and bring in a new way of deeper contextualization. Our departure from the dominant discourse lies in a nuanced and contextualized analysis of the *habitus* or logic of practice of matatu entrepreneurship in Kenya. We hope that the information provided in this book will help to correct some of the tendency of inadequate contextualization of knowledge, technology and practice transfer from one setting to another in transport (Grieco 2012) and in development programmes in general (Easterly 2005, Rodriguez-Pose 2013). Whereas countries such as Kenya aim to develop their transport systems to fit into the globalized transport system (Government of the Republic of Kenya 2007), it may pay for them to remember to also plan for transport for everyday life and within local reach in both urban and rural areas, and not focus mainly on the global flows of people and goods (Robinson 2002, 2008).

The third point of departure is in adopting an entrepreneurship framework to analyze the matatu industry. Whereas the matatu can be studied from different perspectives, an entrepreneurship perspective may provide insights into the structure of this industry. Matatu entrepreneurship has generally been examined within urban transport planning frameworks and rarely as a business in its own right. There are only a few studies such as McCormick et al. (2013) and Kioyi (2011) that have studied the matatu from a true entrepreneurship or business perspective. There are several entrepreneurship frameworks but Shane's individual-opportunity nexus model (Shane 2003) provides a viable conceptual tool to examine how the matatu entrepreneurs discovered and exploited transport demand opportunities at different times and in different places in Kenya. Shane's framework offered an alternative approach that shifted the focus of entrepreneurship research from examining the profiles of entrepreneurs to analyzing the interaction between enterprising individuals and valuable opportunities. The central thesis of the framework is that the entrepreneurship process begins with the discovery and perception of the existence of opportunities: once entrepreneurs perceive or discover opportunities, they develop ideas and strategies on how to exploit these opportunities, leading to key activities of acquisition of resources, designing organizations or modes of opportunity exploitation, and developing and executing a strategy to exploit these opportunities. This process may be repeated over and over again as the opportunities are further refined. While there is the discovery dimension in this process, it is the creative part that turns a potential opportunity into a valued service or a product that consumers are willing to purchase. The entrepreneurship process therefore consists of being found and being made (Venkataraman 2011); a process that Schumpeter (2008) described as creative destruction, which involves destroying and replacing old ways of doing things with new ones, using new methods of production, new marketing outlets, new services, new products and always looking for creative and innovative ways of doing things differently. The creative aspect of entrepreneurship contributes to innovation and socio-economic change. In the chapters that follow, we shall show how matatu entrepreneurs discovered, elaborated, mobilized resources and organized themselves to exploit the transport demand opportunity. Further, we shall show how other enterprising individuals and institutions discovered and exploited opportunities offered by the matatu enterprise.

The exploitation of the matatu business opportunity takes place within the context of the historical political economy of Kenya. The main concern of a political economy analysis is to examine the interaction of political and economic processes in a society (Clark 1998, Department For International Development 2009). Political economy analysis is interdisciplinary in nature, involving perspectives, approaches and methods from diverse disciplines such as Economics, Political Science, Sociology, Planning, Geography, International Relations and Public Health. A political economy analysis can be applied to issues at different geographical, administrative and social units, ranging from households through communities, regions, and nations to an international level. It can also be used to examine a specific problem or issue affecting a sector. Though statistical modelling of the transport service provides insights into the nature of transport service demand and supply, there are other issues that this approach is not able to examine in depth, and which a political economy approach can help to tease out. For example, a political economy analysis is appropriate for examining issues related to decision-making, allocation of resources, distribution of power and wealth between different groups and individuals, the role and influence of different actors, impact of values and ideas, and enforcement of regulations required.

While drawing on the model of entrepreneurial process to examine how the matatu entrepreneurial opportunity was discovered and exploited (Shane 2003), this book pays attention to the political, historical, economic and institutional factors within the matatu sector and the wider Kenyan society that influence the development of matatu entrepreneurship. The central thesis of this book is that matatu entrepreneurship straddles both socio-economic and political spheres of life. Thus, an analysis of matatu entrepreneurship requires not only technical or quantitative aspects but also the social, political and economic issues within and outside the sector. While this book is situated in broader political economy theory, we use appropriate theories and conceptual models to elucidate specific aspects of matatu entrepreneurship as follows:

- an interpretive historical trace of the origin and development of matatu entrepreneurship within the complexity of Kenyan politics, culture and economics (see chapters 3, 4 and 5);
- return on investment and other performance concepts to examine the performance of matatu entrepreneurship (see Chapter 6);
- a logic of practice model to examine the origin and formation of the matatu way of seeing and doing things, and how this process has led to a self-organizing matatu system (see Chapter 7);
- power models and a gender analysis framework to examine some aspects of violence, crime and safety associated with the matatu sector (see Chapter 8);
- innovation theory to examine other creative initiatives in Kenya (see Chapter 9);
- learning organization and organizational learning frameworks to draw out lessons from matatu entrepreneurship (see Chapter 10).

The fourth point of departure is the inclusion of the experiences and voices of operators, owners, users and policy makers to ground the book in lived matatu entrepreneurship and not just presenting facts as told and seen by researchers or policy makers. For a long period of time, transport research published in mainstream journals has tended to transform information collected from respondents to statistical outputs such as correlation or regression coefficients and p-values. Even where information was gathered on travel behaviour, most of it ended up in a travel behaviour statistical model, obscuring the richness and value of narrating the travel behaviour experienced with regard to interaction and use of the travel environment and space. Are we saying that the positivist-quantitative approach that is still largely used in transport research has no relevance? Absolutely not. Our main position is that transport planning and travel experience are multi-dimensional, requiring the use of both positivist-quantitative and interpretive-qualitative approaches. There is a need to get insights from the views and experiences of different people, including operators and users of the transport system as well as policy makers. Getting views from people's experiences is in line with the life story methodology, which views and uses people's stories as fundamental sources of knowledge (Kemuma 2000, 2007). These stories are embedded in day-to-day socio-economic and political contexts as well as different geographical spaces such as the matatu localities. We believe that when people's stories are contextualised they enrich our understanding of the settings within which these stories are embedded. Though personal, when people tell stories they include information about institutions and the contexts that the stories are a part of. Therefore the stories included here are stories about the matatu industry and life in Kenya.

With respect to road safety research, Khayesi (2010) has argued that a consideration of the largely untapped knowledge and views of road users can be part of the process which shifts road safety research from being the exclusive preserve of expert consultants, professional planners and researchers to being a more dynamic field which can benefit from the knowledge and perspectives of a much wider range of people. The extensive criticism of research methods that rely mainly on quantification and statistical model building, largely ignoring qualitative approaches, has partly contributed to the growing efforts to use qualitative methods in transport research. Statistical methods, as pointed out by Jirón (2011:135) "still lack the understanding of the specificity of the experience of travelling for many groups of people, how it impacts their access to urban benefits and how this practice relates to other aspects of urban living". This book therefore contributes to the effort of utlizing situated transport analysis by presenting examples and voices that show how the matatu entrepreneurship is indeed a lived and experienced phenomenon. These experiences and voices are presented in different parts of the chapters. These examples and voices reveal encounters that different people have had with respect to the matatu travel environment, investment, law enforcement and ordinary life in Kenya. As Tuan (2011) has pointed out, human experience of space and place can be direct and intimate, or indirect and conceptual, while mediated by symbols. Whereas there are people who know the matatu industry intimately because of immersion in its activities as operators, owners, mechanics, passengers and traffic law enforcement officers, there are others who know about it remotely from what they have heard or from short encounters with the matatu.

The four points of departure discussed above provide a holistic approach to studying and analyzing matatu entrepreneurship as a self-organizing industry with a distinctive culture and strategies. Though analyzing individual enterprises is important, this focus alone does not bring out fully the way the sector operates as a system, especially how it organizes itself to respond to the demand for a public transport service and by doing so, creating a niche for itself in the public transport system and political economy of Kenya. The research issue that this book addresses is the systemwide functioning of matatu entrepreneurship.

The concept of self-organization has origins in cybernetics, ecology, psychology and computer modelling (Perry 1995, Ashby 2004, Dilts 2014). It has been applied to social or economic phenomena such as the market, the travelling salesman and pedestrian movement (Helbing et al. 2001, Dyer and Ericksen 2005, Schabauer et al. 2005). The self-organization concept refers to the process of order formation in complex dynamic systems (Dilts 2014). As pointed out by Dilts (2014: 1): 'Scientists studying chaos (the absence of order) noticed that when enough interacting elements were brought together, rather than create chaos, order seemed to 'spontaneously' form as a result of the interaction'. The key aspects in the self-organising concept are (Dilts 2014):

- interactions among elements in a system that lead to the creation of a pattern of behaviour;
- the presence of attractors, which act as reference points or anchors, helping to create or hold stable patterns within the system;
- feedback flows, including positive and negative types, which lead to necessary adjustments in the system. The feedback flows make a self-organizing system an open type.

We applied the above elements to the matatu industry and they have helped us to analyse the matatu vehicle not just as a decontextualized, disembodied and lifeless piece of moving metal, carrying people and goods from one place to another, but rather as a self-organizing transport industry, situated in a dynamic transport, socio-economic and political environment in Kenya. We have been able to go beyond the appearance of chaos in the matatu industry to examine the underlying logic of a self-organizing and learning entrepreneurial activity, with an elaborate organizational structure, made up of national and route-based associations, the sustained exploitation of transport demand and diverse business strategies.

A look at the literature on common pool resources and public goods shows that contrary to assumptions about chaos and abuse of such resources and goods due to competition, some local communities have self-organized themselves and devised rules and institutions to manage these resources (Ostrom 2009, 2010). This finding is based on extensive studies of public security, fisheries, irrigation and forests by researchers affiliated to the Workshop in Political Analysis at the University of Indiana (Ostrom 2009, 2010). This research has identified the following as the design principles behind these rules and institutions: clear demarcation of boundaries, application of graduated rules, creation of mechanisms for conflict resolution, building of trust, minimal government recognition and development of lines of communication. These principles are applied to several action situations that bring together actions with individuals who take actions and make decisions based on the information available and an assessment of potential benefits and costs. The point we are highlighting is that the principle of self-organization is not limited to the matatu industry but is also found in other social and ecological resources and services.

How Did We Gather and Analyse Information for this Book?

Authorship of books and scientific work in general tends to be assigned to the person who gathers information and prepares the manuscript. While this approach is justified, we should point out that this book is the outcome of a fairly long process in conceptualization, collaboration among the three of us as authors and other researchers, participation in discussions, involvement in academic meetings and gathering information from different sources. Contextually speaking, the research that formed the basis for this book has been conducted and supported by several people, including sponsors who funded the relevant projects, academic institutions that hosted researchers and the projects, researchers themselves whose work we have drawn upon, research assistants who helped us in several aspects, the matatu experience trajectory that provided a dynamic research context to investigate, and the public that not only pays tax but also uses the matatu vehicles. We have also used theories that have been generated by other scholars. Like other researchers who have gone before us, we humbly acknowledge that we have indeed built on the work of many other scholars and institutions in preparing this book. We see our role in this book as one of synthesizing the available information and providing the reader with a text on the intriguing trajectory of the matatu entrepreneurship experience.

The three of us have been involved in social science research in different settings, for different purposes and from different but complementary perspectives. Along the way, we became interested in matatu industry research alongside our other research projects. Meleckidzedeck Khayesi's research interest in the matatu sector started in 1989 as a mode of transport covered in his MA thesis (Khayesi 1990, 1993, 1995) and developed further in 1995 in a response to a call for research proposals on micro and small enterprises by the Institute for Development Studies, University of Nairobi. He argued for the study of the matatu as a micro and small transport enterprise, especially for the need to examine the terms and conditions of work (Khayesi 1997). This study consolidated and synthesized existing literature and it has provided information used in chapters 3 and 4 of this book that trace the historical development of matatu entrepreneurship. A book chapter on conditions of work was published out of this research (Khayesi 2001a). Khayesi had another interest in the matatu sector from a road safety point of view and he included this aspect in his PhD thesis and related papers (Khayesi 2004, Odero et al. 2003, Khayesi 1999b) and a book (Khayesi 2010). He extended his research focus on matatu, examining the political economy of the sector (Khayesi 1999, 2002), role of social capital in the development of the sector (Kinyanjui and Khayesi 2005), livelihood-safety-matatu link (Nafukho and Khayesi 2002), and opportunities in the matatu industry for transport planning in Nairobi (Kinyanjui and Khayesi 2013).

Fredrick Muyia Nafukho entered matatu industry research from a human resource development perspective when he won a research grant from the Organisation for Social Science Research in Eastern and Southern Africa. He examined driver performance and the risk of road traffic injuries (Nafukho, 2001), and later moved on to assess the link between livelihood and road safety of the sector (Nafukho and Khayesi 2002) and performance improvement (Nafukho and Hinton 2003). Apart from his research interest, Fredrick Nafukho was once an owner of a matatu vehicle.

Joyce Kemuma entered the matatu research from an educational perspective, with a focus on the youthful workforce and its construction of life space through the matatu sector (Kemuma et al. 2002) where she applied Bourdieu's concept of logic of practice and gender as analytical tools. Joyce has extensively used concepts such as *habitus*, among others, in understanding people's ways of thinking, seeing and appreciating certain things as opposed to others and how they consequently respond, make choices and/or act (Kemuma 2000). In her research she has also used gender, intersectionality and discourse analysis in analyzing and contextualizing people's stories from their various positions and situatedness (Kemuma 2012). Joyce brings these analytical tools in contextualizing and understanding the matatu's logic of practice. Like the other two authors, in addition to her research interest, Joyce Kemuma has experienced the development of the matatu in Kenya. Her father owned a matatu that Joyce and her siblings were sometimes asked to operate and she has used this mode of transportation extensively.

Our collaboration therefore brings together diverse research traditions and practical experience to examine the multiple layers in the development of the matatu entrepreneurship in Kenya. We have been assisted in gathering evidence for this book by Alfred Anangwe and Rodney Asilla (see acknowledgments). We also received financial support from Anna Mala towards the continued collection of information from secondary sources. We were greatly motivated by the conversational style used by Dambisa Moyo (2009) in her book *Dead aid: Why aid is not working and how there is another way for Africa.* Her book is also brief, distills substantial information and takes an easy to read approach. We also read and learnt from other books such as Carson (1962), Stiglitz (2002), Obama (2004) and Greene (2012) about synthesizing massive amounts of information and organizing it into key themes in a conversational style. In addition, we benefitted immensely from reading Howard Gardner's (2006) book *The 5 Minds for the Future.* Gardner (2006) argues that to survive in the 21st century, one needs five minds, namely, the disciplined mind which requires us to identify a field of study and dedicate ourselves to it for at least ten years to master the subject matter of the field. One also needs the synthesizing mind, the creating mind, the respectful mind and the ethical mind. Throughout this book, we have relied on the principles in the five minds of the future as to how to synthesize information related to the matatu entrepreneurship. The preparation of this book turned out to be a deep learning experience for us as authors about synthesis, conversational writing style and looking deeply into the matatu entrepreneurship. We are still learning and trying our hands at these issues and hopefully, we shall apply these lessons to other research topics we undertake in future.

Ashgate Publishing not only published the manuscript but also contributed to shaping the book through discussions on the title, content and style. The Transport and Society Series Editor (Margaret Grieco), Commissioning Editor (Katy Crossan), Editorial Assistant (Carolyn Court), Assistant Editor (Margaret Younger) and several staff at Ashgate Publishing provided feedback on drafts of the manuscript as well as administrative support and technical guidance. Their developmental approach to preparing a book manuscript enabled us to progressively improve the quality and content of this book.

In summary, the information used in this book has come from a range of sources that we may categorize as two broad pathways:

- Our own research and publications over the years on the matatu mode of transport and other themes. Our own research included a follow-up or background check through reading reports and general inquiry, to largely complement existing information and also clarify some aspects with little or no empirical evidence, for example, government strategy to phase out the 14-passenger seater matatu, devolution of national governance and implications for planning for the matatu industry, a government strategy to introduce a new electronic system for passengers to pay fares, and the status of umbrella national matatu associations.
- Research conducted by other scholars, which we have drawn upon to extend the frontiers of investigation, building on and tapping into the existing body of knowledge. We maintained contact and/or closely followed the publications of researchers working on the matatu industry/paratransit transport in both Kenya and other countries. We have also drawn on theories and techniques in education, sociology, political science, human resource development, adult learning, and entrepreneurship to help us investigate the emergent features of matatu entrepreneurship. All the sources used are given credit in the text and indicated in the reference list.

We brought our complementary disciplinary strengths to bear on the synthesis and interpretation of the information to develop the themes of this book. Sometimes we would think we had concluded an issue or a section only for one of us to re-read it and point out a gap or some improvement that was needed. For example, we revised the title of the book as well as the structure several times. Any time an issue would be raised, we would go back to the text and refine it as was required, exchanging notes and drafts through e-mails and discussions on the telephone and through Skype. This modern communication technology enabled us to remain in touch though we were based in three different countries. It also helped us to quickly secure literature and information, and interact with several people, located in different places but whose support we needed to prepare this book. We did face some challenges as happens when writing a book. For example, other commitments requiring our attention sometimes caused delays in completing some sections. A frustrating experience occurred to one of us who misplaced a file that had been thoroughly read and corrections made. Despite these few challenges, the entire process of preparing this book has been a fulfilling academic undertaking. As we moved towards completing the manuscript, we even started seeing ourselves as having created our own logic of practice with its unique *habitus* of collaborating via cyberspace and exploring whatever information was available. All these experiences have provided the basis to prepare this book.

Summary

This chapter has outlined the points of departure or the gap in existing literature, the theoretical framework, and methods used for data collection and analysis. The key points in this chapter are as follows:

- There is a need to go beyond the conventional quantitative approach in transport research and embrace qualitative and political economy frameworks in order to provide a holistic approach to studying and analyzing matatu entrepreneurship as a self-organizing industry with a distinctive culture and strategies. Analyzing matatu entrepreneurship and digging deeper to unearth its logic of practice is comparable to peeling off layers of onions.
- The political economy framework and entrepreneurship process model has been found appropriate to help in peeling off the matatu entrepreneurship layers in order to understand how its logic of practice has developed within a dynamic transport, socio-economic and political environment in Kenya. The frameworks have made it possible to offer a nuanced analysis of the matatu public transport service and its embeddedness in society, providing a context-sensitive analysis of informal transport in Kenya. Thus, these frameworks have helped us to move away from seeing the matatu vehicle as decontextualized, disembodied and lifeless piece of moving metal, carrying people and goods from one place to another, but rather as a public transport service that has an underlying logic of practice. These frameworks have also helped us to include the voices of matatu operators, owners and users to provide on-the-ground-reality of matatu entrepreneurship and not just presenting facts as told and seen by researchers in order to provide a context sensitive analysis of informal transport in Kenya.
- Information used in this book has come from diverse sources, including both quantitative and qualitative data, from the work of the authors and other researchers.

Chapter 3

The Roots, Branching and Subsequent Exploitation of Matatu Entrepreneurial Opportunity

Introduction

The growth and dynamics of the matatu transport industry in Kenya is not just in absolute numbers of passengers transported or number of vehicles registered but also in organizational structure, composition of the workforce, extension of links with other sectors, pattern of ownership and geographical spread. The growth has seen an ever increasing number of stakeholders and the matatu entrepreneurship story is one of a process of negotiation and interaction among a number of factors and stakeholders in the national political and economic environment. In its growth path, the matatu business has attracted and intermingled with a number of political and economic interests as well as individuals with diverse socio-economic statuses, often leading to both collaboration and competition in order to secure a niche in the sector. The economic, social and political environmental changes in Kenya since independence have provided opportunities and challenges that matatu owners and operators have responded to as entrepreneurs.

From its early beginnings the matatu tree spread its roots and branched out further in the years that followed. From an entrepreneurial point of view, it is important to examine how this opportunity was discovered and exploited over the years by different stakeholders who have found shelter in different branches of the matatu tree. This chapter examines the roots of matatu entrepreneurship by focusing on the historical and political economy dynamics and how they were leveraged in order to exploit the matatu entrepreneurial opportunity. It then presents snapshots of the key moments that show how transport demand was subsequently developed in Nairobi (Kenya's capital city) and other parts of Kenya.

Entrepreneurial Opportunity

Entrepreneurship is a creative activity that involves making something out of the opportunities available in the environment. As Shane (2003: 4) stated, it 'involves the discovery, evaluation and exploitation of opportunities to introduce new goods and services, ways of organizing, markets, processes, and raw materials through organizing efforts that previously had not existed'. Sometimes, this creative process appears to generate value out of seemingly ordinary life circumstances and even out of things that do not appear to exist or have value or out of challenges that face society. For example, farmers in the Jura region in Switzerland tried to find activities to occupy themselves and to generate a living during the severe winter season. One of the activities they explored was watchmaking. This activity, which was largely based in homesteads, progressively grew from a cottage industry to a major economic activity, largely influencing the planning and development of the watchmaking towns of La Chaux-de-Fonds and Le Locle (Swiss Commission for UNESCO 2012, Kebir and Crevoisier 2008).

The matatu entrepreneurship had its small beginning in the city of Nairobi. Both research and eye witness accounts indicate that matatus surfaced in Nairobi in the 1950s (Kapila et al. 1982). The service is described as having been used mainly by residents of the African residential zones to move goods, as well as people to and from nearby rural areas to their residences in the city (Aduwo 1990). A deeper analysis reveals that the matatu service was a response to a gap in transport demand. In the language of the entrepreneurial process model, the matatu operators identified or discovered this opportunity, organized themselves and started to exploit it. How did this discovery come about?

The initial concentration of the matatu service in African residential areas reflects the inequalities in the Nairobi urban development space that had been created by the colonial state and which has continued to be a feature of the urban history of this city (Murunga 2005). The city was zoned along racial lines, with the zones settled by whites having good basic services and African zones having poor services. The Asian settled zones also had better services than African settled zones. The African settled areas were inadequately catered for by the then existing scheduled bus service. The matatus therefore provided a much needed service to respond to this transport demand. In the beginning, matatu operations charged a standard fare of 30 cents, irrespective of the distance covered. The name matatu is thought to have its root in the Agikuyu phrase, '*mang'otore matatu*', which is translated as "thirty cents", referring to the standard charge (Kapila et al. 1982). There were also a number of rural areas surrounding Nairobi, and the matatu provided a transport service connecting the city and these rural areas.[1]

With political independence in 1963, the new Kenyan state was expected to redress colonial inequity, for example, by allowing Africans to freely move from rural to urban areas. The relaxing of this restriction created new challenges for the independent state. Following the removal of colonial restriction on African movement into Nairobi, the city experienced an influx of migrants (Macharia

---

1   Godard (2007:4) corroborates the important role that informal transport has played in the urbanization of the outskirts of cities in Africa and other developing countries. He noted that 'this type of transport originally provided rural or inter-urban services entering the urban area from the outside. The institutional system of the large mass public transit companies was not able to satisfy all the demand, or respond quickly enough to the rapid urban change which created the major conurbations'.

1987), who could not be adequately catered for with regard to housing, transport, employment and other basic services. The matatus therefore increased in number and geographical coverage in order to respond to the growing transport demand. As Klopp (2012) has pointed out, the impacts of early segregation created land-use and transportation patterns that continue to shape contemporary Nairobi in significant ways. She observes that while on the one hand, the emerging African upper and middle classes found homes in the former European area north-west of the city or in the growing suburbs, all of which entailed heavy reliance on the automobile, which, as in America and elsewhere, is also a status symbol, on the other hand, poorer residents continued to live in the eastern part of the city as well as in informal settlements (Klopp 2012).

Negotiating around the Public Transport Monopoly in Nairobi

Founders of businesses face challenges, which sometimes lead to the death of an otherwise promising venture. The capability of entrepreneurs is thus demonstrated by their ability to handle these challenges. Some of the challenges are unexpected. While there are planning tools that can be used to anticipate challenges and explore possible solutions beforehand, the real test is when the entrepreneurs are in the midst of a true challenge and they have to marshal their intellect and resources to tackle it. Thus, making progress in entrepreneurship and in life in general does not necessarily lie in wishing away problems and challenges but rather in effectively and strategically addressing them, including finding ways of turning adversity into viable solutions (Branson 2009, Collins 2001, Johnson 1999).

Operators of the matatu mode of transport in Nairobi were no exception as they faced a challenge in the form of restrictions. The restrictions arose from trying to penetrate a transport supply that had an operator with a monopoly contract. Whereas the colonial settlement geography and politics of Nairobi led to an unmet transport demand that the matatu operators sought to fulfil, the same process created a transport monopoly. The matatu did not enter a *tabula rasa* transport landscape. There was an existing scheduled bus service operated by a monopoly company known as Kenya Bus Services providing passenger transport. The history of this monopoly is traced to the 1930s, when the need for a public bus service was recognized in Nairobi. To fulfil this need, an agreement was made between the city authorities and Kenya Bus Services, a subsidiary of a United Kingdom-based company known as United Touring Overseas Limited, to provide urban transportation services in Nairobi. United Touring Overseas Limited operated in several countries including the United Kingdom, Sweden, Finland, Portugal, Malawi, Kenya, Australia and New Zealand. The result of this agreement was that Kenya Bus Services was given the exclusive franchise of carrying fare-paying passengers in and around the then Municipality of Nairobi (Aduwo 1990, Khayesi 1997).

Kenya Bus Services is reported to have begun operations in Kenya in 1932 with two buses. It had a transport monopoly in Nairobi, which was renewed in 1985. Its monopoly in transport was given and sustained by Nairobi City Council that had a 25 per cent shares in Kenya Bus Services (Kapila et al. 1982). Given the colonial context, Nairobi City Council, like Kenya Bus Services, was British controlled. The British white settlers and colonial officials, in whose interest the Kenya Bus Services monopoly was maintained, dominated it. Thus, together, Nairobi City Council and Kenya Bus Services subjected the matatu vehicles and personnel to harassment with a view to sustaining their monopoly on public road transport in Nairobi (Ogonda 1976). When the matatus emerged, they were seen as illegal competitors by the Kenya Bus Services management and the local government authorities. This largely explains the harassment the matatu operators faced from Kenya Bus Services and local authorities, especially in the 1960s and early 1970s. Matatus were therefore forced to operate in a clandestine manner (Ogonda 1976).

The contract Kenya Bus Services had with Nairobi City Council was binding and could not be easily dispensed with but the matatu operators went around this issue by exploiting a political strategy using social capital. In 1973, a group of businessmen from Kiambu district is reported to have paid a visit to the late President Mzee Jomo Kenyatta and petitioned him on the status of matatus. Following this visit, the matatu as a public mode of transport and an income-generating opportunity for the poor, received official recognition by a presidential decree (Macharia 1987). The decree allowed them to carry fare-paying passengers and exempted them from the regulation of the Transport Licensing Board, which licensed vehicle operators. The same decree categorized matatus as private vehicles similar to taxis and tourist buses and therefore not subject to Public Service Vehicles licensing. Though the presidential decree contributed to breaking the colonial monopoly of Kenya Bus Services, it initiated an era where the matatu industry had a quasi-legal status and a trend in which their inclusion in policy planning and regulation was ignored. It can be seen that in issuing the decree, the need to regulate matatus was ignored, at least for a while, until 1984 when the Traffic (Amendment) Act was issued.

A consequence of this side-stepping was that 'it took another ten years for the legislation to catch up to the [Kenyatta's] decree, although the planning process still has not done so' (Lee-Smith 1989). A number of researchers concede that this presidential decree was a critical intervention that ended the original illegal status of the matatu, paving the way for its rapid growth in this sector (Kinyanjui and Khayesi 2005, Kemuma et al. 2002, Khayesi 2001, Odero 1997, Ogonda 1992, Macharia 1987, 1997). The granting of the presidential decree needs to be seen partly within the broader political discourse and action on Africanization, a political agenda that was meant to increase the participation of indigenous Kenyans in business and other national development efforts. The matatu operators seem to have drawn on this political logic when seeking the presidential decree. The operators argued that they were using the matatus for self-employment.

The preceding discussion shows how the matatu operators in Kenya organized themselves as a group to present their case to be given official recognition as an informal enterprise that provided employment and income for the poor. This strategy helped these entrepreneurs to break into the monopolistic public transport niche in Nairobi. However, in granting this request, the late President Jomo Kenyatta neither made recourse to nor overlooked the then existing contractual arrangements between Nairobi City Council and Kenya Bus Services.

This case is an example of the role of patron-client relationship in state operation, what Macharia (1997) calls the informalization of the state. It is further noted that the presidential decree even exempted matatu operators from obtaining a trade licence. While on the one hand the matatu operators used social and political networks to secure political support to legitimize their operations, on the other hand, the political establishment also gained in granting the decree to an upcoming middle class that then largely owned the matatus. The number of unemployed persons was also growing in Nairobi. Further, there was a transport problem facing African residential areas. The state therefore secured the support of this middle class and showed its concern about solving problems faced by Africans. In this way, independent Kenya was implementing the Africanization programme. This example reveals how entrepreneurship interacts with the political structure.

The Matatu Tree Spreads its Roots and Branches, 1974–1988

There are three key moments that show the way the seed of matatu transport service presented in the preceding chapter spread its roots and branches in Kenya (see Figure 3.1 and Table 3.1) and the challenges it faced as well as how it tried to solve them or how circumstances led to their resolution. The stakeholders presented in Figure 3.1 and Table 3.1 will be mentioned in different parts of this book but overall, they are diverse groups of people and institutions that have direct and indirect links with the matatu industry.

People and institutions with direct and immediate links, who are generally referred to as primary stakeholders, are owners, drivers, conductors and passengers. Their concerns are with income, employment, safety and accessibility. These issues are examined fully in Chapter 5 which looks at the performance of matatu entrepreneurship. Among people and institutions with indirect links with the matatu, that may be referred to as secondary stakeholders, are traffic police, local authorities, insurance companies, petrol stations and vehicle repair garages. Their main concerns are enforcement of traffic regulations (traffic police) and income generation. In line with the political economy framework adopted for this book, we look at the matatu entrepreneurship as a tree. Its roots are the politics and economy of Kenya. The industry forms the trunk and the various stakeholders take shelter in its branches, exploiting the different opportunities that the matatu industry offers (Figure 3.1).

Table 3.1   Matatu stakeholders and their interests

Stakeholder	Main concern
Matatu owners	Income
Workers: drivers, conductors, stage workers and m*anambas*	Income
Passengers	Safety and accessibility
Other road users: bicyclists, pedestrians, motorists	Safety
Institutions: Local authorities Traffic police Motor vehicle registration unit	 Revenue Driver testing and driving licences Traffic laws Revenue
Businesses: Insurance companies Motor vehicle manufacturers, assemblers and body builder Motor vehicle repairers/garages Petrol stations Driving schools Paint companies Sign writers and scribes	 Income Income Income Income Income Income Income
Bus operators: urban and country buses	Competition for passengers
Politicians	Solidarity support

Source: Khayesi (1999)

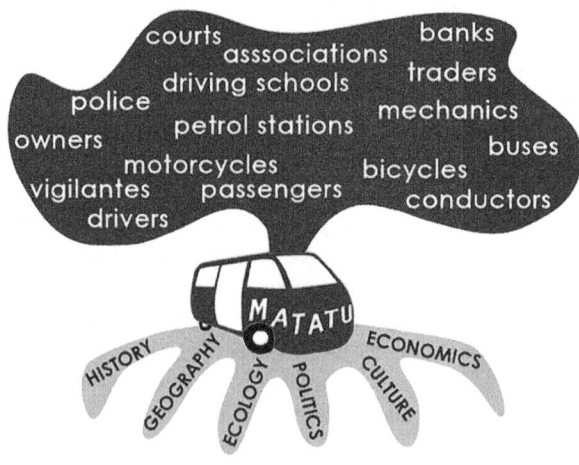

Figure 3.1   Matatu tree

A Matatu Association is Created

The *matatu* industry grew beyond Nairobi to operate in several urban and rural areas of Kenya. In order to coordinate the matatu industry, owners of matatu vehicles formed an association known as the Matatu Vehicle Owners Association. The statement below provides some insight into the role that was expected of this association:

> Seven years ago ... the late President Jomo Kenyatta, repealed the Transport Licensing Board (licenses for private taxis) which legalized matatus. Soon afterwards, matatu operators formed a countrywide organization, the Kenya Matatu Vehicle Owners Association in an effort to 'clean up' the running of private 'taxis' operating in many parts of the republic. Now there are nearly 3,000 matatus carrying passengers in competition with buses and commercial taxis ... . At the moment, passengers in most matatus are still not covered by insurance if there is an accident. What is more, overloading and speed limits are often ignored in the race to squeeze in as many trips, and people, as possible during the peak business hours. And, the 'always room for one more' philosophy continues. Worse still, some drivers have no driving licenses ... (The Weekly Review, 6 February 1981: 11)

The association controlled the operations of the sector and also pressed for their demands. The association had national and branch officials. A new entrant or operator was expected to apply to the association in order to be allocated the route of operation. The association also had a magazine which disseminated information about the industry and welfare of members.

A Legal Effort to Reign in the Matatu Industry: Traffic Amendment Act of 1984

Whereas the 1973 Presidential decree exempted matatu operators from regulation by the Transport Licensing Board and licensing by the Public Service Vehicles Board, over time, it became necessary to bring the sector under some sort of regulatory framework. There are several reasons for this development, including a sustained effort at intensifying state control, involvement of matatu vehicles in road traffic crashes and the need to generate revenue.

In 1984 the parliament of Kenya passed the Traffic Amendment, which was commonly referred to as the Matatu Bill. The purpose of the bill was 'to introduce more stringent controls in respect of vehicles commonly known as matatus' (Republic of Kenya 1984: 400). The Bill covered four main aspects:

- It defined a matatu as a public service vehicle with a seating capacity for not more than 25 passengers, excluding the driver.
- It required matatus to have a Public Service Vehicle Licence and undergo an annual vehicle inspection.

- It specified the minimum age for a matatu driver as 24 years old.
- It indicated that a person needed to have held a driving licence for at least four years before his licence could be endorsed for driving a matatu.

There was an insightful observation in an editorial in *The Weekly Review*:

> At last the government has taken steps to ensure that *matatus* are inspected regularly for roadworthiness. Matatus are here to stay, so the government's new inspection procedures should not be seen as an attempt to do the *matatu* business in. What, however, might work to the detriment of both matatu owners and the public in general could be the introduction into the new inspection system of the kind of corruption which is all too evident in many government inspection procedures, especially in the motor industry (Ng'weno 1984:1).

The matatu operators, represented by the Matatu Vehicle Owners Association, had challenged the introduction of the new bill arguing that it would be costly to meet the requirements and that this could put many operators out of business. The Matatu Vehicle Owners Association tried to ask the government for more time for its members to prepare for the new requirements but the government declined. Matatu operators went on strike in several parts of the country, causing many passengers to be stranded.

Though the enforcement of these regulations has generally been inadequate (Asingo and Mitullah 2005), their introduction in 1984 revealed the role of the state in partly managing the development path of matatu entrepreneurship. In subsequent sections and chapters, we shall show how the matatu operators went about managing these regulations, in some cases by not adhering to them and in others by the state not fully enforcing them.

The Matatu Vehicle Owners Association is Banned

Centralization of state power, which started in the 1960s continued into the 1970s and 1980s in Kenya. Following an attempted coup in 1982, parliament passed a bill that turned Kenya into a one political party state. Though one political party, the Kenya Africa National Union (KANU), had been in power for a long period of time, this bill provided a legal basis for a one-party state, with the aim to silence those opposed to the party. This was a typical situation in a number of African countries in which opposition parties were not allowed to operate for a long period of time, and leaders stayed in power for many years, thereby generating resentment and efforts to remove them through military coups (Meredith 2005). It was towards the end of the 1980s that a wave calling for multiparty politics in Africa gained momentum. However, becoming a one party-state did not silence those who were opposed to or had issues with this form of political management or how Kenya was being managed politically.

The matatu industry has been noted as an important solidarity group that has been used in a number of ways to disseminate political goals and as a tool for politicians (Khayesi 1997, Kinyanjui and Khayesi 2005). This industry has been known to support both the opposition and ruling political elite. As demand for political pluralism increased in Kenya in the late 1980s and early 1990s, the majority of matatu operators who supported the opposition became instrumental in disseminating to the travelling population political messages challenging the establishment through posters and songs (Murunga 1999). Whenever a demonstration was called by the political activists, these matatu operators would join in, paralysing the transport system in the country. At such a time or during these demonstrations, some operators and/or owners feared to offer their vehicles for passenger service lest the vehicles were stoned by rowdy mobs of agitators. Therefore they withdrew their vehicles from the roads. During this pro-democracy agitation and the demonstrations of 1990, the matatu drivers were among the first to greet each other using a two-finger salute, which was a risky thing to do at that time as the salute had the symbolic message of indicating that it was time to have two or more parties and not just one political party in the country.

It can be seen from the preceding paragraph that the matatu industry was affected by the political developments in Kenya in the 1980s. The industry also participated in different ways in the political activities. The matatu sector's engagement in political activities partly led to the state banning the Matatu Vehicle Owners Association in 1987. Among the reasons for the ban were that it provided a path for political activism and destabilized the country, and further that the association had been penetrated by influential rich individuals who were oppressing weak members by, for instance, assigning them to routes that had very few passengers (Khayesi 1997, Kinyanjui and Khayesi 2005). With the banning of the Matatu Vehicle Owners Association in 1987, the government in effect allowed individual operators to operate on any route they chose. While the banning of the matatu association weakened its national reach and role in broader societal issues, a look at documents and discussions at that time show that this association was already experiencing internal management and financial problems as well as external problems, given the fact that a rival organization to the Matatu Vehicle Owners Association had been formed.

Re-organization and Renegotiation in the Matatu Industry, 1989–2001

The struggle for control and regulation of the matatu industry continued despite the official banning of the Matatu Vehicle Owners Association. After the umbrella matatu association was disbanded in 1987, up to about 1991 the matatu stages and ranks were managed by the youth wing group of the then single political party, the Kenya African National Union (KANU) (Khayesi 1997). With multiparty politics being allowed in Kenya towards the end of 1991, some members of the youth wing group became stage workers, not representing a particular political party but serving drivers and conductors and earning a livelihood.

With the dawn of multi-party elections in 1992, the then single ruling political party moved closer to the matatu operators. For example, matatus in Nairobi were allowed by a presidential directive in December 1991 to carry standing passengers, in direct contradiction of traffic requirements (Khayesi 1999). Whereas it may appear that the head of state was responding to the demand for transport in Nairobi, it should be remembered that presidential, parliamentary and civic elections were to be held the following year and this was therefore an act of seducing the operators for their political support and votes.

The 1990s witnessed increasing numbers of business and political groups in the matatu industry. Stage and route matatu workers also organized themselves into 'labour' groups (Khayesi 1997). Strong and competing route-based matatu associations became a key feature of the sector. In 2001, it was estimated that there were 150 membership-route associations in Kenya, 63 of which were in the city of Nairobi.[2] These associations controlled a number of tasks; entry of new operators, regulation and allocation of ranks, day-to-day activities at the ranks and welfare of workers. There also emerged a group known as *Mungiki*[3] that took over the control of certain matatu routes in the city of Nairobi, sometimes leading to violence and even loss of life in ensuing fights between members of this new group on the one hand and matatu operators and security forces on the other hand (Rasmussen 2012). This issue of how the matatu sector is organized is discussed fully in Chapter 4.

There were also efforts to revive a national level matatu association. In this regard, the Matatu Welfare Association was formed in 1997 but not officially registered until August 2001. The aim of the association is to represent the needs and interests of the matatu industry. Details on this association are provided in Chapter 5.

Summary

This chapter has examined how the matatu entrepreneurial opportunity was initially discovered and exploited in the city of Nairobi. It has then traced the key

---

2   This information was provided by an official of Matatu Welfare Association in an interview by one of the authors.

3   Mungiki is a militant group that has been banned in Kenya. Its origin is traced to a religious effort in the 1980s to draw on Agikuyu traditional values to create an alternative to the materialism of Evangelical Christinaity that was dominant in central Kenya (Wamue 2001, Anderson 2002). It is thought that Mungiki emerged as a splinter group within this religious effort that operated under the banner of the 'Tent of the Living God' (Anderson 2002). Rasmussen (2012) reports that when Mungiki members initially entered the matatu industry in the early 1990s, they were only looking for work but they later changed and took over the running of the industry on some routes in Nairobi and in other parts of Kenya.

moments in the further development of the matatu entrepreneurship as it interacted with political, economic and social issues at different periods in Kenya's political economy as well as influencing or being influenced by them. The chapter has been able to provide insights into decisions and strategies of exploiting entrepreneurship deployed by both individuals and groups in Kenya and what the government or state did or did not do. The key points of this chapter are as follows:

- The emergence and entry of the matatu in the transport and urban life of Nairobi revealed a conflict between African indigenous capital and a multinational-dominated urban transport sector. The matatu vehicles were seen as illegal and pirate, infringing on contractual arrangements between Nairobi City Council and Kenya Bus Services for provision of public passenger transport service in Nairobi.
- A presidential decree in 1973 partly helped the matatu entrepreneurs to break this monopoly. Intersection between the matatu industry and politics would remain an important feature of this sector in subsequent years as the chapters that follow will show.
- An important change observed is the transformation of the matatu industry from a small business in the 1960s and early 1970s of one or two persons trying to make ends meet to a major channel of investment for some people in the 1970s and continuing to the present.
- The matatu industry in Kenya stands out as not only a business for employment-creation and income-generation but also as a socio-economic and political arena. The matatu sector then becomes a tool or a means for economic and political influence and it is within this setting that a number of networks and relationships are constructed to achieve multiple and often conflicting interests.
- The development of the matatu entrepreneurship process reveals trends in the evolution of indigenous Kenyan capitalism as expressed through a diversity of actors and businesses that includes the matatu industry.

Chapter 4

Weaving through the Emerging and Changing National Political Landscape, 2002–2013

Introduction

There have been further developments in the exploitation of the matatu entrepreneurship opportunity in the period 2002–2013. Many of the national level structural developments are not completely new but rather a revisiting and re-enacting of previous issues related to control and the relationship among the stakeholders. This chapter examines the recent key moments based on the literature and our personal experiences: renewal of traffic law enforcement, increased efforts at creating a national level umbrella organization for the matatu industry; a new national constitution, a new transport agency and more nuanced matatu business strategies.

Renewal of Traffic Law Enforcement

The new government which came to power in Kenya in 2002 indicated a commitment to improving road safety. It sought to reform the operation of public service vehicles by publishing Legal Notice No.161 in October 2003 (Republic of Kenya 2003; Chitere and Kibua 2004). The legal notice included road safety measures that the government required the relevant agencies to enforce. The specific objectives of the Legal Notice were to: reduce accidents caused by speeding; enhance the safety of commuters; ensure responsibility, accountability and competence of drivers and conductors; eliminate illegal drivers, conductors and criminals that had infiltrated the industry; and facilitate identification of vehicles and restrict their operation to authorized routes (Republic of Kenya 2003, Chitere and Kibua 2004).

The road safety measures that the government set to come into force by 1 February 2004 were:

- fitting of speed governors in all public service vehicles and commercial vehicles whose tare weight exceeded 3,048 kg in order to limit speed to 80 km/h;
- fitting of seat belts on all public, commercial and private vehicles;

- employment of drivers and conductors on a permanent basis;
- issuing of badges to public service vehicle drivers and conductors;
- issuing of uniforms to public service vehicle drivers and conductors;
- indication of route details and painting of a yellow band on each matatu for easy identification;
- re-testing of drivers every two years;
- each driver prominently displaying his or her postcard-sized photograph of their head and shoulders taken without a hat.

The new rules should have come into force in November 2003 but the public transport operators felt that the time given was too short and requested a longer preparation time. There were animated arguments and exchanges between the government and the public transport operators over the new rules. Hon. John Michuki, the then Minister for Transport and Communications, insisted that the new rules had to be implemented after protests from public transport operators, who called for a national strike that was subsequently called off when it became clear that the government was not going to relent (Khayesi 2004).

These rules, commonly referred to as Michuki rules are not entirely new but rather a restatement of the 1984 Traffic Act amendment and other existing traffic regulations under the traffic act. Though there was heightened effort to enforce the rules, it dwindled within a short period of time (Asingo and Mitullah 2005), partly because the minister behind them was moved to another ministry, revealing the inadequate institutionalization of policies and issues. Instead, the policies tend to be linked to an individual. Though matatu operators generally complied with the regulations, there were many instances of lack of compliance. Within a few months of implementation, some studies revealed a number of problems and issues, reflecting inadequate attention paid to the key success elements in implementation (Chitere and Kibua 2004). These included:

- tampering with speedometers by some dishonest operators to enable them to drive the vehicles beyond the authorized speed of 80 km/h.
- seatbelts fitted on some public transport vehicles that were substandard or did not work at all and therefore did not guarantee safety in the event of collisions.
- seatbelts not always being put on by passengers and the conductors not emphasizing their importance unless they suspected that they were about to encounter the police.
- fares being hiked, especially in the first few months of enforcement of the legal notice with the argument that the operational costs for the matatus had increased because of implementing the new road safety measures. The increase in fares inflated the cost of transport for commuters.
- inadequate supply of public transport vehicles following the elimination of unroadworthy vehicles and standing passengers in buses and mini-buses.
- reported laxity in law enforcement.

- reported re-emergence of cartels on some routes.
- media reports of corruption among key government officials in relation to issuance of public service vehicle licences and inspection certificates.
- reported overloading of vehicles in towns such as Nakuru where some matatus still carried 18 passengers instead of the required 14.
- failure of some drivers and conductors to wear their badges or to display their photos.
- touting still being common and some crew members still played music loudly in their vehicles.
- speeding, careless overtaking, overloading in some cases and paying of bribes to the police were commonly practised.
- reports that a number of vehicles having been certified as roadworthy were not actually in good mechanical condition.

The experience with renewed road safety and regulatory framework underscore the need for securing the involvement of all stakeholders, continued high-level of political concern and prioritization, inclusive transport policy and practice, research and evaluation of implementation, and awareness raising, publicity and empowerment (Khayesi 2004). The Kenyan public generally wished that Hon. John Michuki had stayed longer in the ministry and continued to spearhead the implementation of the Legal Notice to reduce road traffic crashes that have continued to kill, maim and injure the travelling public in Kenya (see Chapter 7 for details on road traffic injuries).

A New Constitution and Decentralized Governance

Kenya, like many countries around the world, has had a long walk along her path to democratization (Edward and Hayoz 2014, Edward and Aregay 2014). Since gaining independence from the British colonial government, Kenya has undergone a transition from an authoritarian one-party political system to a multi-party system. The key turning points in the transition path (Edward and Hayoz 2014) include: the independence election in 1963 under the Lancaster House constitution; the dissolution of Kenya African Democratic Union (KADU) and the centralization of power for the presidency; the fall-out of the ruling elite and the formation of Kenya People's Union (KPU) party in 1966; the banning of KPU and the detention of party leaders which marked the end of the short stints of multi-partism in 1969; the death of President Kenyatta and ascension of President Moi to power; the attempted military coup d'etat in 1982; the 'Mulolongo' queue elections in 1988; the re-introduction of multi-party elections in 1992; the Inter-Party Parliamentary Group constitutional amendments and 1997 multi-party elections; the defeat of Kenya African National Union (KANU) in 2002; the general elections of 2007 and post-elections violence in 2007–2008; the formation of a grand coalition government in 2008; and the promulgation of a new constitution after a national referendum in 2010. We shall highlight the recent constitutional change of 2010 and general elections of March 2013 because they introduced new structures that have implications for the governance of the country, including matatu entrepreneurship.

Kenya faced a major threat in her strive for survival as a nation in the 2007 general election. The intervention of the international community through a mediation process led by the former United Nations Secretary General, Kofi Annan, helped to stop the violence that followed the disputed presidential results of the general elections held in December 2007. It also led to the formation of a grand coalition government in which the incumbent and the key opposition candidate shared power. The 2007–2008 events also created an opportunity that enabled the passage of a new constitution on 27 August 2010. The new constitution brought significant democratic changes after over 20 years of unsuccessful attempts at reforming the constitution. The main changes include devolution of political and economic power, entrenchment of the bill of rights and gender affirmative law, an enhanced process and system of selecting peoples' representatives to guarantee free and fair elections, and the introduction of leadership and integrity provisions for public leaders (The Constitution of Kenya 2010).

The constitution has decentralized political power and created institutions and laws that should promote democratization. Constitutional separation of powers and decentralization of government is meant not only to check excessive accumulation and abuse of power by the executive, but also to provide a means of recognizing the legitimate claims of ethnic, tribal or regional entities. Governance structures have also been aligned to the new reforms by the constitution. For instance, a more independent Judiciary that can resist the pressure from the executive arm as well as from the rich and powerful is envisaged in the new constitution. The aim of creating such a judiciary is to guarantee justice to all and provide a mechanism for resolving social-political disputes as well as ensure respect of civic rights by all concerned parties, especially the state. Thus, the new constitution has established the Supreme Court of Kenya as the highest court in the country. This is an independent constitutional body which has exclusive original jurisdiction to hear and determine disputes relating to the elections to the office of President, among other tasks (The Constitution of Kenya 2010). The absence of such a court in the old constitution could have contributed to the outbreak of violence in Kenya following the disputed presidential election in 2007. In the new constitution, the president exercises the executive authority of the Republic, with the assistance of the deputy president and cabinet secretaries under whom the bureaucratic institutions operate but the presidency and the entire executive have very limited discretionary powers now because of the limitations and checks placed by the new constitution on their exercise of authority. For example, the president can now make public bureaucratic and constitutional office appointments subject to a transparent selection process by constitutional bodies and vetting by parliament. This was not the case in the old constitution.

The new constitution also marks a radical departure from the old system by providing for a devolved governance structure. This new structure provides for two levels of governance: national and county. While the executive authority at the national level is exercised by the president, deputy president and cabinet as mentioned earlier, the executive authority of the county is vested in, and exercised by a county executive committee consisting of the county governor and the deputy county governor and members appointed by the county governor, with the approval of the assembly, from among persons who are not members of the assembly. The legislative authority of national government on the other hand is vested in parliament comprising the Senate and the National Assembly. These are two houses as opposed to one house in the old constitution. The legislative authority of a county, on the other hand, is vested in, and exercised by its county assembly. A county assembly is empowered to legislate on matters necessary for the effective performance of the functions and exercise of the powers of the county government, as provided for in the constitution. A county assembly also, while respecting the principle of the separation of powers, is expected to exercise oversight over the county executive committee and any other county executive organ.

While the new constitution carries a great promise for the democratization process in Kenya, it is important to note that it is in its implementation that this promise will be realized. Matatu entrepreneurship is not a mere spectator of these developments. Its owners, operators and passengers have participated in these political developments. The decisions and actions undertaken within the new constitution and governance structures will affect the matatu industry. The way this will happen is not easy to forecast at this early stage but from experience the matatu logic of practice of self-organization and learning will provide the tools with which to negotiate and exploit opportunities offered by the new political developments.

The National Transport and Safety Authority

The National Transport and Safety Authority (NTSA) was formed in April 2013 after the signing into law of the National Transport and Safety Authority Bill in 2012 by the then president, His Excellency President Mwai Kibaki. The mandate of the NTSA is to formulate and implement road transport policies. The specific responsibilities of the NTSA (under the National Transport and Safety Authority Act 2013) include:

- registering and issuing licences to motor vehicles;
- conducting motor vehicle inspection and certification;
- regulating public service vehicles;
- advising the government of Kenya on national policy with regard to road transport sector;
- developing and implementing road safety strategies;
- conducting research and audits on road safety;

- compiling inspection reports relating to traffic accidents;
- establishing systems and procedures for overseeing training, testing and licensing of drivers;
- formulating and reviewing the curriculum of driving schools; and
- coordinating the activities of persons and organizations dealing in matters related to road safety.

Government Initiative to Phase out 14-seater Matatu

In October 2010, through an announcement by the then Minister for Transport, Hon. Amos Kimunya, the government of Kenya revealed a plan to phase out a matatu type that was legally allowed to carry 14 passengers (hereafter referred to as 14-seater matatu) allowing mainly with 25-seater or 38-seater matatus or mini-buses to remain. The reasons for this proposal were as follows:

- To reduce congestion and traffic jams on the roads, especially in major urban areas such as Nairobi, Mombasa and Nakuru. The buses would have a larger capacity, and therefore, fewer of them would be required for public transport, resulting in lower congestion and fewer traffic snarl-ups. The 14-seater matatu was singled out as a key contributor to traffic jams due to the disruptions it causes. Because of its small size, drivers try to weave in and out of flowing traffic, including driving off the road and invading sidewalks (in the few cases where they exist) and even driving in the wrong lane.

Figure 4.1   A picture of matatu vehicles on pedestrian sidewalks

- To reduce air pollution from vehicle gas emissions. Environmental conservation is one of the priority areas in the current Kenyan government's development plan known as Vision 2030 (Government of the Republic of Kenya 2007). A major goal of this plan is to transform Kenya into a middle-level income economy by the year 2030 by pursuing three pillars: social, economic and political. Environmental conservation falls under the social pillar. In an effort to protect water catchment areas and the ozone layer, the government of Kenya has instituted air pollution measures related to industrial gases as well as motor vehicle fuel combustion gases. To this effect, it was thought that by replacing the 14-seater matatu with the 25- and 38-seater buses, there would be fewer vehicles on the road, thereby leading to less pollution that would be harmful to the ozone layer. Another aim was to reduce noise pollution from vehicle engines and loud music normally played in the matatus.

The government announced that it had stopped the issuance of the Transport Licensing Board (TLB) licence for the 14-seater matatus, only allowing the board to issue licences for the larger capacity 25- and 38-seater buses. A TLB licence is a mandatory requirement for any matatu owner seeking to have their vehicle recognized as a Public Service Vehicle (PSV) on Kenyan roads, and is issued by the Kenya Revenue Authority (KRA), which is the country's tax and revenue collection authority. This licence must be renewed annually.

This initiative was supposed to have been implemented by June 2013 when all 14-seater matatus were expected to have stopped operating on Kenyan roads. However, this initiative has not been implemented largely due to the resistance it elicited from various stakeholders, especially the matatu owners. There were a number of concerns on their part for their opposition to this initiative by the government. One of the major reasons advanced for the resistance by the matatu owners was that it would be very expensive to replace 14-seater matatus with the 25- and 38-seater matatus. The average cost of the 14-seater minibus, which are mostly the Toyota Hiace or the Nissan Homy model, is approximately 700,000 to 900,000 Kenyan shillings. On the other hand, the average cost of the bigger 25- and 38-seater buses, which are mostly Isuzu models, is 3.5 to 4 million Kenyan shillings. Such a huge difference in price was presented as a major hurdle for the matatu owners, who strongly argued that they were neither financially prepared for such a venture nor were they capable of handling such an investment at that moment. Most matatu owners argued that they were already struggling to make a decent profit from the 14-seater matatus, and that the phase-out initiative would effectively put most of them out of business. They also argued that the larger buses would also be more expensive to maintain with respect to fuel costs, maintenance and repair of the vehicles as well as the levies the larger capacity vehicles attract compared to the smaller capacity ones, such as the tax-on-purchase charges, insurance levies and the TLB levies. For instance, a 14-seater matatu attracts a monthly insurance fee of 9,100 Kenyan shillings, compared to the bigger 38-seater buses, which attract a monthly insurance fee of 25,000 Kenyan shillings.

There was also the fear of risk of loss of employment, especially for matatu drivers and conductors. A matatu normally operates with a crew of two; the driver, and the conductor whose responsibilities are to collect the fare, and to alert the driver on when to stop for alighting and boarding passengers. With larger-capacity buses on the road and therefore fewer public transport vehicles, this situation would translate into fewer crews on the roads. The result would be loss of employment for a number of people in the matatu industry. This would have far-reaching effects as a number of families in urban as well as in rural areas depend on matatus for their livelihood. The move also raised concerns from some quarters in government, such as legislators and ministers. One notable incident was with the then Minister of Finance, Uhuru Kenyatta (who is now the President of Kenya), who opined that the government initiative was a risky move that would create unemployment among the youth in the country, who form a large part of the employed force in the matatu sub-sector (Muiruri 2012). He therefore urged the government to consider postponing the move to a more convenient time in the future. From a strategy point of view, one may argue that the then minister for finance might have been aiming to endear himself to the matatu sector, to secure its support ahead of the 2013 general election, in which he was a presidential candidate. With this intense pressure, the government halted the initiative to phase out the 14-seater matatu. Although there is no clear, definitive timeline for when the phasing out will be implemented, the matatu owners and operators suspect that the government still intends to push on with the plan to phase out the 14-seater matatus and replace them with the larger 25- and 38-seater buses.

National level Umbrella Organizations and Route-based Associations

There are now three associations representing the matatu industry at a national level. These are the Matatu Owners' Association, the Matatu Welfare Association, and the Matatu Drivers and Conductors Association (Box 4.1). In addition to the national level organizations, there are several route-based associations (Kinyanjui and Khayesi 2005). We made an effort to establish the number of these route-based or smaller associations but were unable to get reliable information. They are spread countrywide and frequently break up with new associations being formed. They all come under one of the two or three national umbrella associations indicated in Box 4.1. Both the national level and route-based matatu institutions play an important role in creating an organizational framework in the matatu industry. Route-based associations have been a feature of the matatu industry from the early days in the 1960s and 1970s (Kapila et al. 1982). There are formal institutions that have continued to influence or play a role in matatu entrepreneurship. Further, there are formal national policies and regulations that touch on the matatu industry, for example, vehicle licensing, road safety, vehicle insurance, vehicle inspection and employment. There are also cartels and criminal gangs that use the matatu industry as an operational basis. Sometimes, these latter groups receive high publicity because of the crime and violence associated with them. However, the organizational structure of the matatu industry is complex, revealing some order and logic (Kinyanjui and Khayesi 2005, Graeff 2009, McCormick et al. 2013), and not necessarily a chaotic sector as some studies and the media tend to portray. The matatu industry is thus a meeting point for both formal and informal institutions, which lose their distinction as they are transformed in the matatu way of acting to ensure the survival of the sector. A detailed analysis of the formation and logic of practice of this structure is provided in Chapter 6.

Box 4.1

National matatu associations: Matatu Owners' Association and Matatu Welfare Association

The Matatu Owners Association (MOA) was formed in April 2003. It brings together various owners of matatu vehicles in Kenya. The main objective of the association is to 'promote the interests of matatu owners through effective lobbying and advocacy' (Matatu Owners Association 2014). It has a chairman and committee members. A second national association known as the Matatu Welfare Association (MWA) was registered in 2001 (McCormick et al. 2012). A third association is known as the Matatu Drivers and Conductors Association (MADCOWA). Taken together, the three associations represent the interests of the owners, give the owners a forum in which to discuss issues that affect the industry, provide some basic control of the industry and liase between the sector and the government (McCormick et al. 2012, Graeff 2009).

Since its inception, the MWA has made contributions to the running of the matatu industry. One such contribution that is often cited has been in its participation in the fight against corruption and bribery on Kenyan roads (Matatu Welfare Association 2014). The association works in partnership with the Kenyan Police on initiatives aimed at reducing corruption such as 'Kitu Kidogo Out Project' (KKOP), which has been funded mainly by USAID. Through this project, the MWA organized training for its members with the objective of teaching them effective anti-corruption interventions skills (Matatu Welfare Association 2014).

The Matatu Owners Association and the Matatu Welfare Association have also made efforts to support the implementation of Legal Notice 161 issued by the Ministry of Transport and Communication in 2003 (see above). There have also been attempts to make the matatus user-friendly; especially with regard to people living with disability. This, for example, has been through trying to improve the design of the matatu vehicle to make it easier for people living with disability to board and alight, as well as training matatu crews about how to help such commuters. The above initiative, for instance, has been through lobbying for the designing of steps on buses, a move inspired by a tour of Europe and observing the efficiency of the public transport system, particularly in The Netherlands. The associations are constantly involved in national debates on matatus, including taking up or even challenging issues that they feel will adversely affect the matatu industry. For example, through matatu Savings and Credit Cooperatives (SACCOs), the drivers and other staff affiliated to these businesses have been able to access credit facilities through partnerships with various financial institutions, with the aim of improving their standards of living.

Though the MOA and the MWA have complementary objectives and responsibilities, as happens in many areas of life, there have been cases of fierce rivalry reported between these two main organizations. The existence of these associations, including their complementary and competitive roles, shows the continued effort to control and carve out space in the multi-million-shilling matatu industry.

Proposed 'cashless' Fare Payment System for Public Service Vehicle Passengers

The use of information and communication technology is widespread in many sectors of the world economy. It involves such services as online shopping for books and household goods as well as computer-supported piloting of aeroplanes. Information and communication technology has also found its way into the matatu industry through the installation of entertainment communication and the use of mobile phones by operators and passengers. Another layer of information and communication technology that may be added to the matatu industry is the move by the Government of Kenya requiring all public service vehicles to install gadgets through which their passengers will pay for their fares using smartcards instead of hard cash (Wanzala 2014). This move represents a new form of electronic payment, which already exists in other services in Kenya, partly made possible by an e-banking system known as M-pesa (see Chapter 8). Digitization is one of the issues discussed in many sectors in Kenya. For example, one of the key selling points for political parties during the last political campaign for national and local elections held in March 2013 was the promise of the improvement of the information and communication technology infrastructure in the country to spur economic growth. The younger generation is generally referred to as dotcom or digital as it has grown up in the digital era.

The new move is not just a verbal proposal by the government; it has been given a legal basis by the issuance of Legal Notice No. 219 in 17 December 2013, requiring all matatu owners to install the cashless fare system by 1 July 2014. As an incentive, the government has introduced a Kshs. 10,000,000 award scheme for excellent performance in installation of the smartcard technology amongst matatu SACCOs. Some bus companies have already adopted a cashless payment system. One such platform is known as the BebaPay, which is offered by Equity Bank, a financial institution in Kenya, which has subsidiaries in the greater East Africa region, in conjunction with Google. Some of the bus companies using the BebaPay include the MOA Compliant, CitiHoppa, Kilele, Shuttle, Zamzam, Unified Poa and Metro Trans. The BebaPay experience has also motivated Kenya Bus Services Management to launch its own *Abiria Card* (Kenya Bus Service Management Ltd 2014).

There are several benefits that may accrue from the proposed 'cashless' payment system. At a basic operational level, it will eliminate some problems associated with hard cash transactions. In Kenyan public service vehicles it is a common occurrence for passengers not to have their change from fare remitted to them in instances where they have given more than the standard charge. The most common explanation for this on the conductors' side is the lack of small change, which refers to cash being available in smaller, easily manageable denominations. The cashless fare system, therefore, would eliminate such losses on the commuters' part, as the smartcard payment wouldn't require change. In addition, matatu owners would also maximize their returns. Most matatu crews or operators are known to remit fare collections only from initial journey start points. Fares collected from passengers who have boarded along the way are rarely remitted to the matatu owners at the end of the day. The cashless fare system would therefore ensure that all fares collected would be duly remitted to the owners of the vehicles. The conductor is also required to issue the passenger with a receipt that indicates the fare paid. The owners of the matatu vehicle will be able to track online payments made in real time and have better control of the flow of cash.

How have matatu operators reacted to this proposal? There is a general resistance to the move by most matatu operators. Though they argue that most passengers still prefer paying their fare in cash to the cashless system, one cannot lose sight of the small benefits that the matatu crew will lose as perhaps an important reason behind the resistance.

Matatu Business Strategies

Matatus, just like any other business, have developed business strategies to help them survive in a market that is highly competitive. One of the strategies we discuss in Box 4.2 is the use of graphics, graffiti and texts on stickers as advertisement and marketing strategies in the industry.

Box 4.2

What are matatu vehicles saying through texts on stickers?

Matatu vehicles in Kenya often have messages on their bodies in form of stickers or texts. They also have drawings of different objects, people and scenes. In addition, conductors often carry small boards showing the routes they operate. The matatu is therefore a dedicated space of communication through drawings, text on stickers and the actions of operators. Matatu operators and owners have often defied circulars from the government requiring them to strip matatu vehicles of graphics and decorations. The operators and owners argue that these decorations are meant to attract passengers.

The messages or themes in this rich dedicated artistic space are diverse, including social education through humorous and entertaining stickers or texts, sensitizing passengers to take steps against speeding, political messages, religious messages, often with scripture quotations from the Bible or other sacred texts, business practices such as informing passengers to pay their fare and relationship messages about interactions among different people. The stickers and texts change constantly, often reflecting developments in politics, sports and experiences and tastes of individual matatu owner. When Michael Jordan, for example, rose to fame as a basketball player, his name was featured on some matatu vehicles in Kenya.

Stickers pass on deeper messages, often accompanied with irony, sarcasm, humour and provocation, some examples (with translation into English where necessary) are as follows:

- Usifungue madirisha, ungetaka upepo ungebebwa na boda boda.
- *Don't open the windows; if you wanted the breeze you should have used a rickshaw.*
- Kama una haraka ungesafiri jana.
- *If you are in a hurry, you should have travelled yesterday.*
- Songea mwenzako starehe ni kwa wheelchair.
- *Make room for fellow passengers, comfort is exclusive to wheelchairs.*
- Kulipa ni lazima. Change ni ukikumbuka.
- *Paying fare is mandatory, getting your change back depends on whether you remember.*
- Ungesikiza mwalimu ukiwa shule saizi ungekua na gari yako.
- *Had you paid attention to your teacher when in school, you would have your own car.*

- Hatusemi wewe ni mnono lakini ukikalia viti mbili LIPIA.
- *We're not saying you are fat but if you occupy two seats, PAY FOR BOTH.*
- Msongee kidogo dere anashuka pale mbele uketi.
- *Make room; the driver is about to alight so you can sit in his place.*
- Heri kununua MATATU kuliko kuoa BIBI Mkorofi!
- *It's better to buy a MATATU, than to marry an insolent wife.*
- Ati hakuna kiti? Kwani hawa wako hapa wamekalia mikebe ya rangi.
- *You don't have a seat? Are these people in here seated on paint tins?*
- Unaringa na haujapimwa.
- *You are so full of yourself, and you're not sure of your HIV status.*
- If the music is too loud then you are too old.
- Unajifanya ngombe ukamuliwe na nani?
- *You're behaving like a cow; who should milk you?*
- Ukitaka kuketi starehe, nunua gari yako!
- *If you want comfort, buy your own car!*
- Unajifanya asali ulambwe na nani?
- *You're behaving like honey; who should lick you?*
- Si ati ni gari haina mbio,jam ndiyo kubwa.
- *It's not that the vehicle isn't moving fast; it's the traffic jam which is huge.*
- Usiharakishe dere … wee ndio umechelewa.
- *Don't rush the driver ... you are the one that's late.*
- Usitoe viatu kwa gari!
- *Don't get out of your shoes while in the vehicle!*
- Juzi sare, jana sare, acha aibu, Lipa leo!
- *The day before, no charges; yesterday, no charges; stop embarassing yourself, pay up today!*
- No idle sitting, please chat with your neighbour.
- We accept cards too.
- Matatu huwa haijai!
- *A matatu never fills to capacity.*
- Women are like matatus, you miss one and catch the next.
- Mbona nipimwe na hakuna dawa?
- *Why should I know my status and yet there is no cure?*
- Dawa ya mapenzi ni kupendana.
- *The cure for love is loving one another.*
- Kila nyani na starehe yake, yako ni gani?
- *Each monkey has their own style, what's yours?*

The matatu industry, like any other industry, has also witnessed growth in business strategies. Most research on the matatu industry has focused on its role in public transport, road safety, conditions of work and violence. Little has been done on assessing the business strategies that the matatu *habitus* has generated. This gap in research has recently been addressed in a study by McCormick et al. (2013) that focused on business strategies of the matatu industry in Nairobi. The study reveals the existence of several elements of a matatu business' strategic behaviour with respect to business ownership, structure and levels of investment; financing; routes and vehicle types; pricing; operations; promotion and advertising; customer relations; and business linkages and networking. The study indicated that the degree of organization ranged from very low to moderate levels of organization (McCormick et al. 2013, 2012). Studies also reveal that matatu operators have continued to form co-operatives and/or route-based associations as a business strategy (Kinyanjui and Khayesi 2005, McCormick et al. 2013).

These findings on business strategies point to the reality that the matatu industry has not only grown in the number of vehicles, customers served, number of employees, number of owners, service provided, operators, amount of money earned daily and monthly and geographical extent but also in its organization as a business that seeks to exploit the transport demand opportunity. It should also be noted that with the expansion of the matatu industry, there has been a general decline in scheduled bus services in Nairobi and other towns. This decline which has also occurred in several other African cities is attributed to the withdrawal of government subsidies, increased population, poor management and stiff competition from informal public transport service (Behrens 2011).

Summary

This chapter has examined interaction between matatu entrepreneurship and recent political developments in the period 2002–2013. These developments are still unfolding and we hope that the overview provided here will be examined further in future research. The key points of this chapter are as follows:

- renewed efforts to enforce traffic laws have been part of the reform agenda of the government that took power in Kenya in 2002, as well as of previous governments;
- there have been further national developments in terms of a new constitution, decentralization of political power and creation of a new transport and safety agency; and
- there has been a refinement of matatu business strategies.

Chapter 5
Matatu Entrepreneurship Performance

Introduction

The previous two chapters have traced key moments in the development of matatu entrepreneurship. This chapter goes a step further to examine the performance of matatu entrepreneurship. One of the major goals of starting a business is to grow and make a profit. Matatu operators, like other entrepreneurs in Kenya and other countries, indicate their main objectives of starting this business as being employment creation and income-generation as well as providing a vital transport service to the public and contributing to the overall development of Kenya. Whether looked at from the matatu entrepreneurs' or entrepreneurship literature perspective, there are indicators for assessing performance that we can use in this chapter. The performance of an enterprise can be assessed using the following measurements: survival, growth and employment, profitability and experiencing an initial public offering (Shane 2003). Each of these indicators is explained in the relevant sections below and information provided to illustrate the performance of matatu entrepreneurship. Both quantitative and qualitative data are presented.

Survival

We shall start off by clarifying the concept of survival. This concept refers to the continuation of entrepreneurial effort (Shane 2003). One of the challenges any new initiative faces is the ability to develop beyond the inception phase. This challenge faces nations, states, institutions, companies and enterprises. There are many initiatives in the world that never grew beyond the first step. Some appeared to have started well but died off within a short period of time. Some never went beyond the conceptual stage. They have remained promising ideas on paper but not on the ground. There are many great ideas in the world in the form of resolutions and recommendations but many are yet to be implemented. However, there are some initiatives that have weathered challenges to become success stories. For example, the Grameen Bank started off in Bangladesh as a small initiative by an individual and has grown to become a global model for providing financial support to the poor (Yunus 2007). The wise saying, 'many are called but few are chosen', therefore applies to many initiatives.

Though the death of several individual matatu businesses has been experienced, the matatu sector as a whole has survived several threats on its development path as has been shown in chapters 3 and 4. There are three key indicators of its survival that we explain here. The first is the challenge of legality. In the beginning, the matatu operators in Nairobi had no legal mandate as there was already a bus company that had a contract with the Nairobi city council to provide a transport service. The matatu business therefore started off as an illegal undertaking. Through strategic negotiation and due to a favourable political environment, the matatu operators received a presidential decree exempting them from obtaining a licence from the Transport Licensing Board. The sector therefore survived a major legal challenge. It has over the years weathered several challenges such as rival organizations and the struggle for control both within and without the sector. Some of the strategies it has utilized in sustaining its survival are organizing itself into national and route-based associations, and creating links with several institutions and sectors in society. As explained by Rasmussen (2012), the matatu industry in Kenya has created its own system in which the relationships between formal and informal or state and non-state are constantly being shaped and reshaped.

The second indicator of matatu survival is the increased role it has played in delivering a fare-paying transport service in Kenya. The matatu has spread from the original geographical location of Nairobi to other parts of Kenya. The matatu industry has a large share of passenger transport in Kenya. For example, in Nairobi, matatus are used in 29 per cent of daily trips[1] (see Table 5.1). While it is not easy to get an acurate number, matatu associations generally estimate that there are 80,000 matatu vehicles in Kenya, with 20,000 in Nairobi and 60,000 in the rest of the country. It is possible that the number could be less (may be 60,000 in the entire country) or more but the point we are underscoring is that matatu vehicles form a substantial part of the public passenger fleet in Kenya.

Table 5.1   Trip composition by travel mode in Nairobi

Mode	Percentage
Walking	47
Matatu	29
Private car/taxi/truck	15.3
Bus	3.7
School or college bus	3.1
Two-wheeled mode	1.2
Train	0.4
Other	0.2

Source: Irungu (2007: 5)

1   This type of analysis of determining the propotion of people or travellers and volume of goods using different modes of transport is an important aspect in transport analysis and planning. The results presented in Table 5.1 are generally referred to as modal split or modal share.

The number of vehicles registered as matatus has generally been on the increase with the exception of a few years such as 2011 (Table 5.2). There was a notable significant drop of 87.5 per cent in the registration of mini buses and/ or matatus from 3,600 units in 2010 to 451 units in 2011 (Government of Kenya 2012). This drop was largely attributed to the intended government policy aimed at phasing out the 14-seater Public Service vehicles to decongest major cities. While the number of registered matatus declined, the number of registered buses and/or coaches increased from 1,264 units in 2010 to 1,662 units in 2011 (Republic of Kenya 2012).

Table 5.2   Kenya: number of road licences issued for freight and passenger transport vehicles, 2007–2011

Type of vehicle	2007	2008	2009	2010	2011
PSV matatus	41,219	55,042	11,668	16,199	15,198
PSV buses	8,545	10,219	1,826	6,676	5,692
Freight transport vehicles	30,128	33,407	-	-	-
PSV mini buses	-	-	2,341	5,965	2,790
Total	79,892	98,668	15,835	28,840	23,680

Source: Republic of Kenya (2012:218)

In some rural and urban areas, the matatu was for a long period of time the main public transport passenger carrier until recently when bicycle and motorcycle passenger services developed. Nevertheless, the matatu remains a key mode of transport for both short-distance and long-distance passenger and freight transport in many parts of Kenya (see Box 5.1). As noted by Alila et al. (2007: 297):

> It is not unusual to see an overloaded matatu, not just passengers but also goods. This is a common feature in the rural distribution system as well as for itinerary trading systems. Indeed, most urban and rural retailers of agricultural and households goods use this mode of transport to transport their wares. The rates paid on matatus are based on the distance and the bulkiness of the commodity being transported.

Box 5.1

A visitor to Kenya tells of her experience and perspective on the matatu mode of transport

For years I had heard about the matatu from my husband and friends. Riding in one was going to be one of the adventures of my first visit to Kenya. I imagined they were minivans loaded with people, some sitting on the window ledges, honking their horns as they frantically wove through traffic. I imagined personalized vehicles hand painted with favourite pictures or local idioms to attract the attention of prospective passengers. Some of my images were true, but some were overdramatized. The images may have been true 20 years ago, but most matatus are much less of an adventure today.

The Nairobi matatu seems to be the official vehicle of the middle class worker. The buses are loaded with office workers going to or from work, lots of suit coats and blazers. Don't get me wrong; tourists are welcome. Conductors are very helpful, but it would have been overwhelming without my husband, a Kenyan. My husband knew where the matatus collected in town and their general routes. I was overwhelmed. Similar to US cities, each appears to run a set route and they are numbered but there is no map or guide at the stop with the routes on it. Each conductor holds a sign, but the names of the neighbourhoods don't mean anything to me. The conductors are very friendly and helpful, but their goal is to fill up their bus and get moving. Office workers do that efficiently, tourists like me do not.

The first time we used a matatu, we got on one with three seats left, just enough for our family. Two of the available seats were in front next to the driver, and my husband suggested my daughter and I sit there. It was a good idea until I realized there was no way I was going to make the three foot climb into that seat. It was like getting into a semi truck without the foot step. Therefore my daughter and husband took the two fronts. I got in the back, a more typical step in, although space is not wasted on wide aisles. The seat available, like any bus, was the centre of the very back seat. As I made my way back, I got a few curious glances. My shopping bags and walking shorts didn't match the office attire of the rest of the bus. I would have stood out even if I wasn't a white American, although that was obvious to them too. I was glad it wasn't rush hour, then the conductor fills the narrow aisle with people too, but this was before most folks got off work. Once the bus was full, two taps on the outside from the conductor, and the driver moved into traffic. They stay at the downtown stop until they fill up. I don't know if they are getting behind schedule because there doesn't seem to be a schedule. Yet, there are enough matatus that there seems to be one to take its place the minute it leaves. The next day when we were taking it back into town, one came about every minute so if one was full it just passes by. We were only the second stop out of downtown so they may not come as frequently in suburbia, but there is virtually no waiting near downtown.

The conductor began collecting fares in the front and my husband paid for me. The conductor kept track so he waved me off long before he was collecting in the back of the bus. One courteous passenger proceeded to the door early enough before his stop to pay his fare and not make the other passengers wait. The conductor makes change and gives a receipt. It's a flat fare whether you ride six blocks or 60, although no Kenyan would ride for only six blocks.

Matatus are not US city buses; some are converted vans. There are no yellow lines you must stand behind. You can sit next to the driver in the front seat; conductors make change for your fare. No one puts their bags on the seat hoping you won't sit with them. Drivers wait at the stop if they see you are coming from across the street. Even though it was unfamiliar, it felt a lot kinder than US buses. People come before schedules.

In the village, the matatu is everyone's vehicle and it's a bit less structured. I thought 'here I will see the real matatus' and have my adventure. Yet, they too were less colourful than I expected. Each was personalized with a saying on the back, but their base colour was uniform white with gold trim. I loved reading the sayings on the back and concluded there are more Christian than Muslim matatu drivers. I saw many that said phrases in Swahili that they were protected by God. I saw only one that said Allah provides.

The driver values an extra fare more than the personal space of the passengers so they can be very overfilled by American standards. Yet, the last one who wants to ride would rather pile in than wait for the next vehicle. This was more like I imagined. I got to see the 'real thing' when I saw a beat up one driving down the street with packages on top. It was loaded with people, the sliding door was wide open, and one guy was holding on in the doorway. This turned out to be the exception, not the norm on our trip.

In US culture, we have inefficient bus systems in most towns and cities, and everyone feels the need for at least two cars per family. In contrast, the efficiency of the Kenyan matatu system makes me think we could live comfortably there without a car or at least with only one car. I could see many families finding it efficient enough to not want to assume the debt burden of a car. From an environmental standpoint, they are way ahead of us. I cringe when I'm on a US freeway alone in my vehicle among hundreds of big vehicles with only one person in them. It's so inefficient and environmentally wrong. Most Kenyans use the matatus. They're much more energy efficient. Instead of feeling sorry for people for not owning a car, I was proud that these were my relatives.

Source: provided by a visitor to Kenya in a personal story freely given to Fredrick Nafukho

The third indicator of survival is that the matatu industry has kept on improving a number of elements in order to serve the needs of its diverse market. The improvements include:

- increasing the carrying capacity by introducing vehicles of different sizes. The earliest matatu vehicles were basically saloon cars, carrying 5–10 passengers. The vehicle size has changed over the years to 14-passenger, 25-passenger, 35-passenger and over 50-passenger matatu vehicles. Thus, the matatu vehicles come in different forms, with a mix of small and large vehicles, and varied technological modifications; some of the vehicles are really buses;
- providing better and comfortable seats in some vehicles (but generally the operators put more seats in a vehicle which would otherwise be carrying ten people in order to carry 14 people or more;
- providing entertainment in the form of television, video movies and music in some vehicles;
- streamlining money collection in some vehicles and on some routes;
- adopting new communication technology, for example, using a mobile phone to coordinate their operations;
- offering WiFi and Internet services;
- controlling overloading in some vehicles and on some routes. Overloading of matatu vehicles is still a problem but a few operators have tried to adhere to the stipulated legal limit on the number of passengers to be carried.

Interestingly, the Kenya Bus Services has recently introduced small-size vehicles for carrying passengers on some routes in Nairobi. For a long period of time, this company operated only large buses, each with a passenger capacity of over 50 persons. The legal passenger capacity is always overlooked as it is common for these buses to be overloaded. However, many passengers prefer a safe and comfortable bus environment. Kenya Bus Services has responded to this need by adopting buses that are well managed, without overloading and with a clear list of fares to be paid. This development reflects the need for changes in service provision. The small or mini-bus may be finding its way into the planning and decision-making in a large bus service company since small buses are probably easy to fill up and may also be more effective as a money-generating public service vehicle. Perhaps, this development illustrates Schumacher's (1993) argument that small may be beautiful in some situations, instead of large organizations and structures as the case has tended to be in economic development planning. What is intriguing in this development is the mix of different vehicles by both the Kenya Bus Services and matatu sector. While some matatu operators are moving to buses, the Kenya Bus Services is introducing small buses on some routes.

Figure 5.1   Kenya Bus Services small-sized bus

Growth and Employment

The second performance indicator is growth, which refers to an increase in a new venture's employment or sales (Shane 2003:5–6). We shall examine employment in the matatu industry as it does not have sales as is the case in enterprises such as a retail business. Matatu owners employ drivers and conductors to operate their vehicles. There are two types of drivers or operators in the matatu industry:

- owner-operator where the owner of the vehicle is also the driver and is involved in driving the vehicle on a daily basis;
- hired or employed driver, whereby the owner employs a driver and the owner may be involved in other employment elsewhere.

Studies conducted in the 1980s and recently show that each matatu generally employs two people directly. These are the driver and the conductor. In addition to these two, there are many stage and route workers. Most of these other workers have no direct contracts with matatu owners, drivers or riders. They however have some understanding with the owners and matatu crews. Khayesi (2001a) has given a detailed description of the role of this group of workers in the matatu sector in Kenya, who mainly beckon passengers, sell tickets, load luggage, and sit in empty vehicles to lure passengers. As passengers enter the vehicle, the matatu stage workers begin to leave one by one.[2] They also clean vehicles, manage and control passenger queues, especially at peak hours; regulate the inflow and outflow of vehicles, including assigning positions at the ranks; keep off 'pirate' vehicles (not recognized members at a specific stage or on a route); relieve conductors and drivers; and run errands for drivers and conductors. These tasks are related to customer care, regulation and keeping of law and order or gate keeping and warding off intruders as well as vehicle maintenance. The stage workers generally get payment from drivers, riders and conductors for performing these tasks. The stage workers organize themselves into labour groups and even have officials or leaders. They charge money from every vehicle that uses the ranks where they are based. The intriguing question is: 'How is it that these groups of workers are able to exercise influence and extract cash from matatu operators when there is no written contract in place?' The answer partly lies in the existence of a strong social network that these groups form. The other reason is the political support that the stage workers can draw upon when the need arises. They use both legal and illegal means to extract financial resources from the sector.

There are of course a number of issues regarding the conditions and environment of work, in particular:

- the prevalence of verbal contracts, which is about 80 per cent as indicated in some studies (see for instance Kinyanjui and Khayesi 2005, Nafukho 2001). This means that drivers and conductors can be dismissed by owners for both major and minor reasons. The dominance of verbal contracts and their temporary nature is not limited to the matatu industry but also exists with the employment of house helps (Mutisya 1995), coffee and tea plantation workers (Mwagiru 1997) and informal sector workers in general furniture making (Kinyanjui 1996);
- the amount and nature of payment, with many matatu workers being paid primarily on a daily basis. A number of workers who have been interviewed during research indicate that their pay is low. These workers use varied and alternative strategies to get additional money, including reliance on earnings by their partner, business, keeping back some of the money collected from passengers, support from friends, farming and savings;
- long working hours for the crew, estimated at 9–12 hours per day (Nafukho and Khayesi 2002, see Box 5.2);
- uncooperative and rude passengers and colleagues;
- poor vehicle maintenance by owners;

---

2   There are several stories about passengers who entered a matatu vehicle filled with these matatu stage workers. These passengers often thought the vehicles were about to start off but to their surprise, the vehicle did not and it actually took longer to fill. In some cases, these travellers, eager to reach their destinations, found out that they were perhaps the first 'true' passengers.

- open stages and inadequate protection from hot and rainy weather conditions;
- passengers complaining about lost luggage;
- harassment from traffic police officers and local government officials;
- lack of worker medical and retirement benefits (Khayesi 1997);
- infiltration of the sector by criminals and cartels (Mutongi 2006, Rasmussen 2012);
- general public negative attitude and perception of the matatu industry (Mutongi 2006);
- pollution from vehicles and the general environment, including noise pollution, exhaust fumes, particulate matter and smoking, which affect the health of the operators and general public (van Vliet and Kinney 2007);
- the risk of road traffic collisions, which affects the matatu workers, passengers and other road users (see Chapter 7).

Box 5.2

Working hours in the matatu industry

Matatu workers generally work long hours, largely in the range of 9 to 15 hours per day although there is notable variation. The drivers and the conductors generally work 13 to 15 hours and the stage workers 9 to 12 hours. In order of relative importance, the drivers work the longest, followed by conductors, stage workers and others.

This pattern of distribution arises due to the nature of tasks in the matatu industry. The driver has to go in the morning to collect the vehicle from the owner's home or the parking place for the night. He or she also has to take the vehicle back at the end of the day. The conductor may not necessarily be with the driver during the very first part of the day. There is also a tendency to recruit a conductor on a daily basis. This means that the driver will not always work with the same conductor on most days. The stage workers report directly at the stage and leave early when the number of passengers begins to decline. In fact, at most stages, there are very few stage workers after 8:00 pm in the evening.

Source: Khayesi (1997)

The importance of employment opportunities offered by the matatu industry has to be seen against a background of an increase in the number of people, especially young people looking for employment and limited employment opportunities. In Kenya, as in many countries of the world, the unemployment rate refers to the number of people actively looking for a job as a percentage of the labour force.

The unemployment rate in Kenya has averaged 22.4 per cent in recent years but had risen to 40 per cent by December 2011 (Republic of Kenya 2012). The number of people actively looking for employment in Kenya is estimated to be 18 million (Republic of Kenya, 2011). It is estimated that the number of new jobs created in the modern or formal sector increased from 56,300 in 2009 to 62,600 in 2010, accounting for 12.4 per cent of total jobs. The total number of self-employed and unpaid family workers within the modern sector was estimated to have increased from 67,500 in 2009 to 69,800 in 2010. The informal sector[3] contributed 80.6 per cent of jobs in 2010, that is, about 8,829,900 persons in 2010, up from 8,388,900 persons engaged in 2009, an increase of 5.3 per cent (see Table 5.3). Nairobi province still commands the largest share of informal sector employment, estimated at 24.7 per cent, followed by Rift-Valley and Central provinces with 18.8 per cent and 15.8 per cent respectively (Republic of Kenya 2011).

Youth unemployment in Kenya negatively impacts the economy since an unproductive labour force leads to lost output in terms of goods and services produced and consumed. Youth unemployment also has a social cost in terms of indirect health costs, illicit activities which lead to increased insecurity especially in urban areas like Nairobi, Mombasa, Nakuru and Eldoret.

The emergence and growth in the number of matatus in Kenya has played an important role in addressing the youth unemployment problem. Matatu enterprise has changed the mindset of many Kenyan youths challenging the convention that employment has to be created by the government in a formal work setting. Many Kenyans, including the young. have been enabled by the matatu business to become drivers, matatu workers and many others have become their own bosses

Table 5.3   Employment in formal and informal sectors in Kenya, 2006–2010

	2006	2007	2008	2009	2010
Wage employees in modern establishments in rural and urban areas	1857600	1909800	1943900	2000100	2060400
Self-employed and unpaid family workers	67200	67500	67400	67500	69800
Informal sector	7068600	7501600	7942300	8388900	8829800
Total	8993400	9478900	9953600	10456500	10960000

Source: Republic of Kenya (2011:69)

---

3   In Kenya, the informal sector generally refers to all small-scale activities that are normally semi-organized, unregulated, and use low and simple technologies, while employing few persons. It is generally thought that the ease of entry and exit into this sector, coupled with the use of low level or no technology makes it an avenue for employment creation.

by owning successful matatus. Matatu workers include men, very few women, youth and other age groups, as well as single and married people.

The results of a study conducted on working conditions in Nairobi, Thika and Ruiru in the 1990s revealed that matatu work is a male-dominated activity (Table 5.4). Out of the 263 workers interviewed, only one (0.4%) was a woman. The rest (262 or 99.6%) were men. There were 107 drivers (40.7%), 81 conductors (30.8%), 67 stage workers (25.5%) and 8 others (3%). A recent study on the matatu industry in Nairobi found out that out of 200 operators interviewed, only 6.7% were women and the remaining 86% were men (Kioy 2011:11).

Table 5.4   **Distribution of matatu workers by sex**

Sex	Drivers	Conductors	Stage Workers	Others	Total	%
Men	107	81	66	8	262	99.6
Women	0	0	1	0	1	0.4
Total	107	81	67	8	263	100
%	40.7	30.8	25.5	3.0	100	

Source: Khayesi (1997)

The majority of workers (187 or 71.1%) in the same study were married men (Table 5.5). Only 75 (or 28.5%) stated that they were single. One driver did not state his marital status. The drivers had the highest number (92 out of 107 or 86%) of respondents who were married. The highest number of respondents who were single (39 out of 81 or 48.1%) was among the conductors. One of the driver respondents indicated that owners of *matatus* prefer married drivers. The reason for this preference, he explained, is that a married driver is seen as responsible and reliable because he has children and a wife to support. Due to this social responsibility, such a driver can stay in one *matatu* longer than a driver who is single. More drivers were married compared to conductors and stage workers (Table 5.6). Marital status partly gives an indication of dependency rate, which is one of the reasons that may lead to a search for a job. A recent study conducted by Kioy (2011:11) found that out of 150 respondents who participated in a survey, only 36 (24%) were single and the rest (114 or 76%) were married. Kioyi (2011) also found that the need to support families was commonly cited by these respondents as one of the reasons for entering matatu business.

Table 5.5   Marital status of matatu workers

Marital Status	Drivers	Conductors	Stage Workers	Others	Total	%
Single	14	39	19	33	75	28.5
Married	92	42	48	5	187	71.1
No response	1	0	0	0	1	0.4
Total	107	81	67	8	263	100
%	40.7	30.8	25.5	3.0	100	

Source: Khayesi (1997)

The workers in this study were organized into the age groups 25–29 (79 out 263 or 30%) and 30–34 (72 out of 263 or 27.4%) (Table 5.6). There are, however, noticeable variations among the workers. The drivers are concentrated in the age groups 25–29 (27 out 107 or 25.2%), 30–34 (34 out 107 or 31.8%) and 35–39 (25 out 107 or 23.4%). On the other hand, the conductors are concentrated in the age groups 20–24 (31 out 81 or 38.3%) and 25–29 (29 out 81 or 35.8%). The stage workers are concentrated in the age groups 25–29 (20 out 67 or 29.9%) and 30–34 (25 out of 67 or 37.3%). The age distribution among the workers reveals that they are at the prime of their lives. This is the general age at which people in Kenya begin formal employment after school. A recent stdy by Kioy (2011) found that 48% of 150 respondents operating in the matatu industry in Nairobi were 26–35 years old. The agedistribution of the rest was as follows: 12% were 18–25 years old, 30% were 36–45 years old and 8% were 46–55 years old (Kioy 2011:18).

Table 5.6   Age of matatu workers

Age Group	Drivers	Conductors	Stage Workers	Others	Total	%
15–19	0	5	1	0	6	2.3
20–24	2	31	11	1	45	17.1
25–29	27	29	20	3	79	30.0
30–34	34	11	25	2	72	27.4
35–39	25	3	6	0	34	12.9
40–44	9	0	2	0	11	4.2
45–49	2	2	0	0	4	1.5
50–54	2	0	0	1	3	1.1
55–59	2	0	0	0	2	0.8
60+	3	0	0	0	3	1.1
Unknown	1	0	2	0	3	1.1
No response	0	0	0	1	1	0.4
Total	107	81	67	8	263	99.9
%	40.7	30.8	25.5	3.0	100.0	

Source: Khayesi (1997)

Profit

The third measure of performance is profit, which refers to surplus of revenue over costs (Shane 2003: 6). Generally, the ability to make a profit or generate income is a key concern in entrepreneurship. As a matter of fact, this aspect is extensively analyzed in entrepreneurship literature. Sales and employment are the commonly used indicators to measure profitability and return on investment (Shane 2003). In the context of matatu entrepreneurship, return on investment can appropriately be looked at in terms of private rates of return and social rates of return.

By private rates of return, we are referring to profits that accrue to matatu owners as a result of their investment which is in the form of financial profits received on a daily basis (see Box 5.3). Based on our discussions with individual matatu owners, they shared with us stories of success where they noted that owning a matatu is like owning a milk cow which you are always prepared to milk in the morning, mid-day and evening. In the case of matatus, successful owners pointed out to us that money always came in the morning, lunch time and in the evening especially those operating in large cities such as Nairobi, Mombasa, Nakuru or Eldoret. In some cases, the matatu is the main business investment for some people and in others it is one of the many business ventures for some entrepreneurs.

Box 5.3

Private rate of return: a mix of success and failure cases of matatu investment

The cases presented in this box are available on the Internet. With permission from the author, we are able to present them to illustrate the experience of investors in matatu entrepreneurship.

The first experience is of a senior police officer who had seen a business opportunity and went for it. Back then, he was two steps below the rank he currently holds, meaning; he had more spare time to manage a side business and still be able to provide – service to all   as the police slogan indicates. He took a loan from a saving and credit cooperative society (SACCO) within the force and took another loan from his bank. With the money, he bought a 14-seater matatu. It was a step in the right direction for the officer of law and four years later, he owned seven 14-seater Matatus. His success in the transport business seemed to go hand in hand with his job performance and at the prime of building his business empire, he was called by the state to serve in a more demanding position. His new position took most of his time and as much as he would have liked to continue running things in the matatu business, he could not find the time. He hired a manager for his matatu business and in less than a year he had

---

sold the last of his seven vehicles. Although the police officer did not make a loss considering the amount of money he had invested and how much he had in his account at the time of winding up, it was not his desire to close the business. He still dreams of owning a transport company with a fleet of more than 30 vehicles. The author of this story notes that he is one of many that have tried their hand in the business and reaped the fruits.

The second is the experience of an investor who has been in the matatu business for over 15 years. He started his business in Kikuyu town, near Nairobi, in the early 1990s where he owned two Mitsubishi colts T120. He sold his two mini matatus popularly known as Tung'othi and bought a new Nissan matatu. He moved his investment from the rural area and came to the city where he managed to build an empire and a trademark that still sells today. He personally hires staff and manages his fleet on a daily basis.

A third case is the experience of a prominent Nairobi lawyer. He started with one bus not very long time ago and has managed to build one of the most respected transport service providers. Today, he commands over ten buses and over 30 employees. His success is plainly attributed to his dedication to his job and a no nonsense approach to corruption and the rule of law. A fourth one is a private investor who had a fleet of over ten vehicles. He is said to have received a rude shock after the people he had hired to manage his investment turned to making merry with his earnings and became popular at the local bars as the biggest spenders in beer and nyama choma. His investment was on the brink of going under when he fired the managers and relocated to another town.

Source: Wambururu's Blog (2014)

In terms of the value of the matatu industry, a typical 14-seater matatu van that is often bought second hand in Kenya or directly from Japan costs just over Kshs. 1 million (US$ 12 820) and a 37-seater mini-bus costs Kshs. 3.8 million (70 per cent of the matatus commonly referred to as 'Nissans' were valued at Kshs. 50 billion (US$ 48 718) (McCormick et al. 2013). These figures are always on the increase as more matatus are purchased. The profitability of the matatu industry can be supported by the fact that there are individuals in Kenya who borrowed from banks, cooperatives, friends or family to start with one matatu and ended up owning a fleet of matatus and even transitioned from matatus to owning several buses and business in real estate (see Box 5.3). In Kenya, for example, one will see fleets of matatus with similar trademarks such as Wepesi Express, Webuye Escort, Rift Valley Cross Roads, Mount Kenya Express, Manyanga Express, Eldoret Express and Mwembe Tayari Express just but to mention a few. Mostly, matatu vehicles with a similar name are owned by one person or a group of people.

Matatu owners interviewed in studies indicate that they have utilized the income from this business to invest further in activities such as farming, shops, savings, residential houses, the matatu business itself (e.g. increasing number of vehicles) and other transport business (e.g. moving from matatu to bus transport and/or lorries). Owners and workers also indicate that they use income from the matatu to financially support their families and other dependants by meeting basic needs such paying school fees, buying clothes, buying food and paying rent (Khayesi 1997, Kioy 2011).

A Kenyan national micro and small enterprise baseline survey conducted in 1999 included transport enterprises. There were 13,257 transport enterprises in urban areas and 6,905 in rural areas, forming a total of 20,162 (1.6%) enterprises of the entire sample. As shown in Table 5.7, the matatu and/or bus passenger contributed to employment of 7,752 workers.

Table 5.7   Distribution of transport micro and small enterprises

Activity	Total Workers	Total Enterprises	Employee mean monthly income (Kshs)
Ship and boat building and repair	3,456	1,7727	6,000
Motorcycle and bicycle assembly	1,192	596	12,250
Motor vehicles	1,125	281	-
Oil and petrol	564	563	9,014
Urban, suburban, inter-urban highway passenger bus/matatu	7,752	2,567	14,142
Other passenger land transport, including taxis	8,218	7,840	3,856
Freight transport by road	4,524	1,405	43,333
Ox cart, donkey cart and hand cart	6,909	3,451	6,892
Construction materials transport, e.g., sand, stones	2,904	580	71,330
Supporting services to water transport	94	281	20,000
Services incidental to transport N.E.C	281	281	3,000
Repair motor vehicles and motor cycles	13,726	4,633	16,656
Repair bicycles	12,102	8,944	3,676
Total for all MSEs surveyed	2,361,250	1,289,012	-

Source: Central Bureau of Statistics, International Centre for Economic Growth and K-Rep Holdings Ltd (1999:87–89)

Though we have provided examples of positive private rate of return, there are stories about entrepreneurs who incurred losses in the matatu business. They did not get the profits they expected and some even withdrew from the business. This situation arises due to several reasons (Kioy 2011, Khayesi 2001a): which include:

- a matatu vehicle being involved in a collision and being written off;
- a matatu vehicle being destroyed during a strike;
- a matatu vehicle being stolen;
- an increase in costs of operation;
- dishonest drivers and conductors who do not give all the money collected to the owner, cheating on the amount spent on fuel and other operational costs; and
- poor management of cash-flow by owners who may lack financial management skills.

In the case of social rates of return, these are benefits that accrue to society at large based on investments made in matatus. These benefits include a transport service which enables employees and students to reach work and school in time as well as paying taxes. Though the modal split reveals the share of matatu in overall passenger transport, it does not tell the full story of matatu travel experience (see Box 5.4). The real life stories is in how the matatu helps people fulfil important functions and roles of going to work, school, market, funeral and burial ceremonies, political meetings, weddings, hospital and or visiting a grandparent's home. There are several workers and people in rural and urban areas who cannot imagine travelling to work and for other purposes without the matatu services. The key role of the matatu in transporting workers is often revealed when there is a strike by the matatu workers. Many people who commute to work using matatus are forced to walk long distances or look for lifts or car pool or just stay at home.

Box 5.4

Matatu travel experience and accessibility for many passengers

The saying 'what you do, you understand' is one that can be applied with a plethora of experiences especially when it comes to describing matatu travel experience to an individual who has never had such an experience. It is only upon embarking on the adventure; that is travelling in a matatu, that this quote can be properly fulfilled. The matatu is a flexible taxi that attracts more and more customers, and is never full and keeps on adding more and more passengers to the extent that some will precariously hang out on the back door (in the case of a box matatu) or the side door (in the case of a min-van or min-bus), as it heads for a specific destination. Cheaper, faster, flying, flexible, convenient, and inevitable, matatus are a must for some commuters because of their accessibility to certain roads unreachable by buses especially in sub-urban, rural, and remote rural areas of Kenya. Travelling in a matatu is an experience that leaves one with a mixture of emotions: excitement, exhaustion, annoyance, liveliness, fun, tiredness, amusement, education and entertainment in the case of those with music.* The inclusion of informality within the formality influences the emotions conveyed upon this journey. The formal structure of the type of matatu and the workers, mixed with the informality of the differing passengers, destinations, conversations, music and thrilling or questionable adventures along the way emphasizes the experience that is travelling in a matatu. Visitors travelling to Kenya, often leave the country with several humorous stories about their experience in a matatu. Reflecting on this travelling mode therefore leaves passengers with unforgettable memories.

Each matatu trip contains the ability to create an exhilarating life experience. The inclusion of thrilling scenery, unforgettable escapades with fellow passengers, music, matatu crew, laughter and general excitement surrounding the matatu travel only emphasizes this unique travelling experience. While Germany may have its Mercedes Benz Taxis, New Delhi its Tuku Tukus, London its red Buses, and New York its Yellow Cabs, Kenya's matatus are a distinct part of its culture and a staple within the Kenyan society. An American colleague to one of the authors of this book and who was travelling to Kenya for the first time was asked what kind of new thing she planned to do while in Kenya. She reflected for some time and responded that the matatu travel experience was what she was looking forward to. When asked why, she noted that all her friends who had been to Kenya always talked about the matatu travel experience. In addition, she mentioned that she had read a lot of stories about the matatu and its culture. She had also heard stories from other Americans who had visited Kenya who had recounted their travel experiences with the matatu (see Box 5.2 for her matatu travel experience).

Note: *The matatu travel experience is entertaining in itself, even without music.
Source: Reflections by authors

Matatu owners also pay municipal taxes, licence registration fees and government taxes (Table 5.8). Besides the government estimates provided in the earlier sections of this chapter, the data presented in Table 5.9 come from research studies focusing on costs and benefit of the matatu industry. As shown in the table, the matatu provides both direct and indirect benefits to the economy such as job creation, tax revenue to the central and county governments, employment creation for individuals working in the *jua kali*[4] industry and who repair matatus,

4   This Kiswahili word literally translated as 'hot sun' is generally used to refer to the informal sector in Kenya.

Table 5.8   Economic costs and benefits of the matatu industry in Kenya

Issue	Benefits	Costs
Employment provided by over 40,000 Matatus in 2004	80,000 direct jobs 80,000 indirect jobs	High direct and indirect costs of operating a matatu
Taxes	Industry pays over Ksh. 1.09 billion per annum to the Government in taxes	High tax burden, 135% of vehicle value excluding VAT on motor vehicles
Insurance	Annual collection in premiums Kshs. 4 billion	Accident and theft risks are very high
Reliable transport means and pollution	Provides a reliable from of transport to commuters which also benefits employers	The cost to society arising from emissions of old (more than 8 years) vehicles as well as their disposal where they eventually become junk is enormous. Noise pollution and inconvenience to the public
Income and traffic Rules	Provides income to the owners who are private entrepreneurs	Total lack of adherence to traffic rules, prescribed routes, and regulatory requirements.

Sources: Kimani, Kibua and Masinde (2004), McCormick et al. (2013)

and income revenue to the matatu owners who save or invest in other economic activities such as real estate, education of their children or family members, and health sectors. Besides the benefits accruing to investment in the matatu industry there are direct and indirect costs associated with the industry. For instance, the highest direct cost of the matatu industry to the Kenyan economy is the problem of road crashes which leads to loss of human life and the human capital needed to develop the country. In some parts of the country, matatus are a big problem to road safety since many of them do not adhere to traffic rules, prescribed routes, and regulatory requirements.

Another social return rate from matatu investments can be explained in terms of benefits that financial institutions such as banks, cooperative societies and other micro-lending institutions derive from their lending to matatu owners. Because of the existence of the matatus, financial institutions are able to increase the volume of lending which helps grow the Kenyan economy at large. There are also cases of matatu drivers and stage managers who have ended up becoming matatu owners themselves from the daily collections and earnings made. Vehicle spare part business owners greatly benefit from the matatu industry since matatus are driven at very high speeds and require daily maintenance hence the need for spare parts on a daily basis. The poor roads in many parts of the country also lead to a very high depreciation in the matatus and so the high demand for spare parts. The *kali* industry has also been thriving ever since the matatu appeared in Kenya because the mechanics are flexible and always willing to provide quick service to matatu drivers when called upon. They have the capability to provide service to matatus at any time anywhere whenever contacted by the matatu operators. Thus, matatus heavily depend on the *jua kali* mechanics for vehicle maintenance, service and repairs.

Initial Public Offering

This aspect of performance refers to the sale of stock to the public (Shane 2003:6). We checked literature and enquired to find out if any individual or a group of matatu owners has been able to sell stock to the public. For example, we checked if the matatu industry is listed on Nairobi Securities Exchange Limited (formely known as Nairobi Stock Exchange Limited). This indicator of performance seems not to have been realized in the matatu sector. However, there are matatus organized as Savings and Credit Cooperative Societies (SACCOs). Some of the matatu SACCOs are well organized and they represent an effort by members to invest or have shares in the matatu industry. Perhaps some of the SACCOs will sell stock to the public in future or be listed on the Nairobi Securities Exchange Ltd. Paratransit transport operators in Dar es Salaam and Cape Town are being encouraged to form companies to participate in shareholding as service providers in rapid bus transit systems (see Chapter 9).

Summary

The following are the key points from this chapter:

- The matatu industry benefits directly and indirectly a number of individuals in Kenya and has transformed not only informal rural and urban transport, but also people's lives in numerous ways.
- The transformative nature of the matatu in Kenya has been noticed by both people within and without the country. Ask any tourist to Kenya what they remember most about Kenya and the answer will most likely be the matatu. The authors of this book have met many visitors who have been to Kenya who have always talked about the matatu travel experience and its transformative abilities.
- The performance matatu entrepreneurship cannot be captured in pecuniary terms alone, but also in non-pecuniary terms.

Chapter 6
The Logic of Practice of Matatu Entrepreneurship as a Self-Organizing Sector

Introduction

In the previous chapters, we described how the matatu sector has evolved as a self-organizing sector over more than 50 years to become a formidable and ever-increasing multifaceted organization in its structure, composition, extension to other sectors, stakeholders involved, pattern of ownership and geographical extent. These chapters also reveal a sector that has historically, politically and economically struggled for its existence and recognition and whose growth has been achieved largely through competition and to some extent, organization and collaboration. We also understand that matatu entrepreneurship has been moulded and remoulded through negotiation and interaction processes involving different factors and stakeholders with a number of political and economic interests as well as individuals with diverse socio-economic and political statuses and interests. This experience gives a picture of the matatu as a self-organizing informal mode of public transport entrenched within the Kenyan political, economic and social arena, where the politics of the time, who knows who (social capital), and economic capital have played crucial roles. Also revealed is how the different factors and stakeholders involved in the shaping of the sector were also shaped by the political, economic and social changes in Kenya from the colonial period to the present. This consequently creates vitality in the matatu sector in as far as it pertains to discovery, exploitation, expansion and performance in terms of survival, growth, profitability, employment and even how it touches and affects the day to day lives of Kenyans in the public and even private front. Clearly, we are looking at a sector that has developed its ways of seeing, appreciating certain types of vehicles and ways of doing things, blurring the distinction between formal and informal sectors.

This chapter takes the discussion further by not only examining how the interaction of formal and informal players with a number of interest groups and individuals has led to the emergence, regulation and control of matatu as a self-organizing sector in Kenya but also offering a deeper contextualization by employing Bourdieu's sociological theory of the logic of practice (Bourdieu's 1990). By using the theory of logic of practice and interlaced concepts such as field, *habitus*, economic and social capital (who knows who), the chapter shows how the history, politics and economy of time, stakeholders' social, political and economic positions has had significance in influencing and shaping a matatu business-related *habitus* and subsequently the logic of practice of a self-organizing sector in the fare-paying-passenger transportation field in Kenya; a field that is dynamic, contested and marred by politics and violence. Chapter 7 offers an in-depth analysis and discussion on violence and security. In this chapter, we establish the logic behind the matatu practice as a self-organizing industry and argue that this logic is fundamental in explicating the crucial strategy in the industry. Some researchers have referred to the matatu business as madness but upon careful analysis, we realize that though there may be chaos or violence, the matatu industry has developed some kind of a matatu-field-specific *habitus* with a logic of practice. A recent study by Rasmussen (2012) discusses the inside system of the matatu industry, showing that being in the matatu system is not the same as operating within the law. We therefore take what Rasmussen calls the matatu system further by examining the underlying logic of practice in this industry as a system, which sometimes operates within the law but mostly out with the law.

Practical Logic, Logic of Practice and the Role of *habitus* According to Bourdieu

Pierre Bourdieu was Professor of Sociology at the College de France. He developed theoretical and analytical frameworks to understand human behaviour and multifaceted living conditions. Central to Bourdieu's sociological work is the concept of a logic of practice that underscores the importance of people and practices within the social world. To Bourdieu, social agents operate using an often taken-for-granted implicit practical logic; the so called practical sense. According to Bourdieu (1990:86), 'practice has a logic which is not that of the logician. This has to be acknowledged in order to avoid asking of it for more logic than it can give, thereby condemning oneself either to wring incoherencies out of it or to thrust a forced coherence upon it'. Bourdieu continues to expand on logic of practice by stating:

> This practical logic – practical in both senses – is able to organize all thoughts, perceptions and actions by means of a few generative principles, which are closely interrelated and constitute a practically integrated whole, only because its whole economy, based on the principle of the economy of logic, presupposes a sacrifice of rigour for the sake of simplicity and generality and because it finds in 'polythesis' the conditions required for successful use of polysemy (Bourdieu 1990: 86).

The logic of practice, according to Bourdieu, is then connected to a field-specific-*habitus*, which means that the practice and its logic come into existence through a field-specific-*habitus*. The same field is the one that produces field-specific-*habitus*:

> The conditions associated to a particular class of conditions of existence produce *habitus*, systems of durable, transposable dispositions, structured structures predisposed to function as structuring structures, that is, as principles which

generate and organize practices and representations that can be objectively adapted to their outcomes without presupposing a conscious aiming at the ends or an express mastery of the operations necessary in order to attain them. Objectively "regulated" and "regular" without being in any way the product of obedience to rules, they can be collectively orchestrated without being the product of the organizing action of a conductor (Bourdieu 1990: 53).

The *habitus* produced by conditions associated to any field become norms producing and guiding practices. This is the *modus operandi* that functions in a handy way in accordance to the norms of the field characterized by certain ways of thinking, feeling, acting and classifying the social world and their location within it.

Jenkins (1992) argues that Bourdieu constructed a *theoretical* model of social practice which is time and space related. This practice, according to Bourdieu, is not consciously or wholly consciously organised. Though not consciously planned, practice however 'happens' because it embodies a practical logic – something Bourdieu likens to a 'feel for the game', which works 'outside conscious control and discourse' (Bourdieu 1990: 61). To be exact, human beings take themselves and the social world around them for granted. In other words, we do not think about what we do because we do not have to. By emphasizing the logic of practice, Bourdieu endeavours to capture the 'intentionality without intention' (Bourdieu and Wacquant 1992: 19). Bourdieu refers to the taken-for-granted aspect of social practice as 'doxic experience'; that is, 'coincidence of objective structures and internalised structures' (Bourdieu 1990: 20). Jenkins likens Bourdieu's idea to that of Giddens (1984) who also underscores the fact that much of the daily life that humans are involved in is undertaken automatically and habitually by means of what he calls 'practical consciousness'. Bourdieu also states that social life, in all its fullness and intricacy, is not simply achieved on a tenet-managed basis. To Bourdieu, practice has a fundamentally creative nature and a fuzzy logic, and as such undertakings employed commensurate with the logic of practice, do not and cannot necessarily have the orderly and well-groomed orderliness of bearing expected from normative or juridical principles (Wacquant 1992: 22).

Though Bourdieu argues that practice is organised in a way that lacks conscious thought it has a rationale and/or practical intention. This element of practice not only underscores that individuals have goals and interests, but also situates the foundation of their practice in their own experience of reality or their practical logic.

Looking at Matatu Entrepreneurship Practice with the Help of Bourdieu's Theory of Practice

Bourdieu in his theory of logic of practice uses concepts that we find useful in analyzing the matatu sector. In this chapter, the matatu sector is conceptualized and analyzed as a field within the fare-paying-passenger-transportation field in Kenya. The concept of field, used in this chapter, refers to 'a relatively autonomous social microcosm' governed by 'specific logics' (Brubaker, 1993: 22). As a field, the matatu sector is a locus of struggles and competition for the right to exist in space with regard to having access to terminals and routes and being part of the fare-paying-passenger sector within a larger field of fare-paying-passenger transport system in Kenya. Bourdieu argues that a particular field generates and assumes specific forms of interest making it a system of real interactions between positions or stakeholders. As is the case with any field, the basis of matatu as a field or a community of practice is the collective belief in its base as a fare-paying-passenger mode of transport. We therefore identify, analyze and interpret the matatu's '... field-specific stakes, the particular forms of interest, capital and power, the pursuits of which constitutes the fundamental dynamic of all fields' (Brubaker, 1993:223). As a field, the matatu industry has a logic of its own created by conditions of existence within the field and the surrounding factors and stakeholders affecting it.

We also see the matatu industry as a practice with a practical logic and/or a logic of practice. This sector, it is argued has developed a matatu-related *habitus* which has subsequently created a unique matatu *modus operandi*. Other concepts borrowed from Bourdieu used in this book are largely derived from capital namely; economic capital referring to money and other physical asserts, and social capital which has to do with rewards or special treatment given by virtue of some existing affiliations between individuals and groups.

In applying the arguments in the foregoing section on *practical logic, logic of practice and the role of habitus according to Bourdieu* to the matatu sector as a field within the fare-paying-passenger-transportation-field in Kenya, some crucial issues begin to appear. It therefore becomes viable to contend that much of what we usually and automatically refer to as matatu-related behaviour – itself an analytical or second-order construct – is in fact, when viewed in the context of the matatu actors' daily lives, part and parcel of a practical rather than an abstract logic. In other words, matatu-related behaviour is itself a practice of everyday matatu related life, something which is intertwined with its very organisation, guided by a practical or implicit logic.

Formation of the Matatu *habitus* and Logic of Practice

Chapters 3–5 identified a number of key moments in the growth path of matatu entrepreneurship. This path of growth was not a mere passing encounter but also the process of creating the matatu logic of practice. In the sections that follow, we demonstrate how the matatu logic of practice was produced and reproduced at these key moments.

Marginalization and the Genesis of Matatu Logic of Practice

It was shown in Chapter 3 that Kenya was colonized by the British. What is important from a logic of practice perspective is the effect of new lifestyles introduced during the colonial period on indigenous Kenyans, especially those in the urban areas, who had lost their land and forms of livelihood. These people were now forced to work in newly created clerical and/or manual work leading to a need for transport from their homes in rural areas or informal urban settlements to their places of work in urban areas. Given the existing political, economic and social disparity created, supported and maintained by the colonial powers with a logic of practice based on race and class, the indigenous Kenyans were poor and without means of transport. Matatu services therefore came to exist due to the new political order of segregating people along different zones based on race and economic class. In Nairobi, the white-settled zones had the best transport services, followed by the Asian settled zones. These zones were well served by the then existing scheduled bus service but the zones for indigenous Kenyans had poor services or no services at all; a gap in the transport service or demand that matatus responded to. This need and gap in transport demand for the poor Kenyans became acute, especially in Nairobi. At this point, economic capital crucial in the introduction of matatus was a rare commodity among the Kenyans ranked as the lowest race, based on whiteness ideology of superiority. The few Kenyan owners of matatu vehicles were those with some economic capital who saw the need and acted in a space of vulnerability in the 1950s in Nairobi where the first matatu vehicles appeared. Their economic capital and audacity of hope (Obama 2006) saw the beginning of a self-organizing sector as well as a genesis of its logic of practice, unique to its beginning from marginal spaces and positioning in the Kenyan political, economic and social arena. The sector was started by a few economically able Kenyans who were determined to serve the economically less fortunate Kenyans. The marginality that the owners and passengers shared, probably prompted the matatu owners to charge a standard fare of 30 cents. This was a fare that those in need of this kind of transport service could afford. The matatu service was mainly used by indigenous Kenyans from racially segregated zones and the nearby rural areas to get to their work places and residential areas in the city.

Though the matatu vehicles and the Kenyan passengers were marginalized on the basis that this was a mode of transport for the 'colonized blacks and economically disadvantaged other', the business was also marginalized because the colonial powers privileged the Kenya Bus Company owned by the British Transport Company through a monopoly contract signed in the 1930s giving Kenya Bus Service Ltd exclusive right as the only mode of transportation for fare-paying-passengers in and around the Municipality of Nairobi. As a consequence, matatu owners right from the onset, battled for recognition and inclusion. This brings the question of economic capital, social capital and contention in the public transportation for fare-paying passengers as a field. The Nairobi City Council (NCC) constituted of British white colonial officials and settlers, who by using economic and social capital gave the Kenya Bus Service Ltd to a British multi-national company (who at the time also had the economic capital) to run such services. This was a challenge to the survival of the matatu, an unrecognized mode of transport, which at the time lacked the kind of economic and social capital that the British white colonial officials and settlers had. Perceived as illegal competitors, the matatus experienced marginalization as they struggled for inclusion at this point in history, where the white-settler-dominated local government authorities NCC and KBS had the power and monopoly. With the existing monopoly, the fare-paying-passengers-transportation field became a contested field between matatus as a mode of transport representing the Kenyan indigenous people with meagre economic and social capital and the privileged multinational-dominated urban transport sector. As a beleaguered and marginalized mode of transport by the Kenya Bus Service Ltd and local authorities up to the 1970s, matatus operated from marginal spaces in a secretive manner in order to survive. The clandestine manner in which the matatus operated was actually the beginning of a *modus operandi* unique to a marginalized and harassed field.

Struggle for Recognition from Margin Spaces, Growth, and Alignment of the Logic of Practice

Chapters 3–5 have provided details on the historical development of matatu entrepreneurship. In this section, we discuss historical moments when and how matatu operators from spaces of marginality aligned the matatu logic of practice further. The first historical moment was in securing a presidential decree that allowed matatus to operate without a licence from the Transport Licensing Board. The year 1973 became a milestone after a group of businessmen from Kiambu district, a district that the late President Jomo Kenyatta came from, approached him regarding the status of matatus. As a result of the petition, matatus gained an official recognition through a presidential decree which legally allowed matatus to carry fare-paying passengers. The president sympathized with the matatu operators and exempted matatus from the following: (1) the regulation of the Transport Licensing Board (TLB), which licensed vehicle operators, (2) Public Service Vehicles (PSV) licensing since recognized matatus were classified as private vehicles similar to taxis and tourist buses, and (3) their operators from obtaining a trade licence. This decree led to the expansion of the matatu sector in Nairobi and other parts of Kenya. In Nairobi, however, matatus continued working from marginal spaces since the decree did not remove the contract between Nairobi City Council and Kenya Bus Service. The businessmen, we argue based on a logic of practice theory, used shared Kikuyu ethnicity and language (Kikuyu as mother tongue) as a social capital shared with the president, and used their positions as businessmen, with economic capital to secure political support and legitimization of the matatu sector. The president in turn used the businessmen's economic capital and their position as an upcoming middle class as a win-win situation because the matatu business offered employment and filled the transport gap that still existed. These exemptions inevitably positioned matatus as a quasi-legal sector in the transport field not covered by planning policies and regulations. This exemption meant that the matatu as a marginalized self-governing sector continued with their *habitus* and *modus operandi* which they reinforced as they continued to create their own set of rules until 1984 when the Traffic Amendment Act or Matatu Bill was issued.

The second historical moment is how the matatu operators circumvented adherence to the Traffic Amendment Bill of 1984. Whereas the bill restricted seating capacity, introduced a Public Service Vehicle Licence, introduced a mandatory annual vehicle inspection and set 24 years of age and at least four years of experience as the criteria for someone to be employed as a matatu driver, in principle, matatu's *modus operandi* with a logic of their own was only temporarily interrupted. Due to corruption, the traffic police who were to see to it that the law was enforced demanded for *chai*.[1] Many matatu drivers paid bribes and continued overloading their vehicles while those who were not willing to pay changed routes at high speed at times causing fatal crashes. Abundance of bribery and laxity from the government to enforce the laws sustained an anarchist way of doing things in the matatu sector. This defiant self, which became a part of matatu *habitus*, was nurtured and upheld because a number of matatus were actually owned by people who in one way or the other worked in the government or had networks with policemen and others who provided them with protection subsequently reinforcing a matatu logic of practice with the cartel-like behalf. A repeat of the same process of defeating a renewed effort at enforcing traffic laws was noted in 2004. The government reintroduced road safety measures from the 1984 Traffic Act amendment and other existing traffic regulations under the traffic act but these measures were questioned by the public transport operators who argued that the Minister for Transport and Communications' demand for the immediate enforcement of the measures was unrealistic (Republic of Kenya 2003, Chitere and Kibua 2004). Though the Minister for Transport and Communications was eager to enforce the regulations, there was no sincere commitment from all the law enforcement bodies. As soon as the then minister behind the reintroduction of safety measures was moved to another ministry the regulations were once again disregarded (Asingo and Mitullah 2005). In fact, many matatu operators had obeyed the regulations half-heartedly (Chitere and Kibua 2004). Given the government's laissez-faire attitude towards the matatu *modus operandi* and logic of practice, even reinforcing it, it is not surprising that traffic regulations have not been fully enforced.

The third historical moment is the creation of matatu associations. Matatu associations have been a feature of the industry from its early days. In the initial period, small route associations were formed. However, as the matatu industry expanded to other urban and rural areas in Kenya, there arose a need to coordinate the industry among matatu owners. The Matatu Vehicle Owners Association (MVOA) was thus formed to manage as well as advocate for the sector at national and local levels. As a managerial body, MVOA received applications from new matatu owners and allocated routes of operation. As advocate and activist, the association, for example, challenged the 1984 bill recommendations which they

---

1   This Kiswahili word literally means tea. However, it is also used occasionally to refer to a bribe, especially when those involved want to disguise what they are talking about.

argued were costly and feared that this would subsequently put many operators out of business. To reinforce their demands, they called for strikes to put pressure on the government for more time for its members to be ready to meet the new requirements but the government declined (Ng'weno 1984). This was a sector that had created and embodied a matatu business *habitus* with a logic of their own which they were not prepared to lose. Due to the involvement of matatu owners and other staff in expressing and supporting dissenting views from the KANU government in the 1980s, the government banned MVOA in 1987 (Khayesi 1997, Kinyanjui and Khayesi 2005) but the struggle to keep the matatu *modus operandi* continued and saw a resurgence of a new association in 1997 (formally registered in 2001). Due to the existence of different shareholders, there emerged conflicts involving different route-based *matatu* associations which were formed after MVOA was banned (Khayesi 1997).

The process described above shows the deep interconnectedness of the matatu sector with different stakeholders (as presented in Figure 3.1 and Table 3.1 in Chapter 3) that have all in one way or the other influenced the matatu logic of practice.

Summary

This chapter has traced and discussed the matatu logic of practice in relation to the matatu conditions of existence, conditions that have contributed to the creation of this logic. The matatu sector as a fare-paying-passengers field within a larger field of fare-paying-passenger transport system and within the Kenyan wider political, economic and social context is at the centre of struggles and competition with and from different stakeholders and interest groups. The key points of the chapter are as follows:

- The circumstances associated with the matatu sector conditions of existence in Kenya have produced matatu *habitus* and norms that have in turn produced the matatu logic of practice. The players in the matatu industry in Kenya have evolved their own sets of rules, structures and ways of doing things in order to secure economic survival and maintain control.
- The matatu entrepreneurship has developed an elaborate self-organizing system consisting of associations, contracts, regulations and mechanisms for relating with the state.
- The matatu position, as clearly depicted in the matatu tree presented in Chapter 3, shows how this sector has struggled to exist, and how the government and politicians have all in one way or the other contributed to the logic of practice, a logic which according to Bourdieu is not the logic of the logician.

Chapter 7
Violence, Crime and Safety

Introduction

The preceding chapters have shown the contribution of the matatu industry to accessibility, employment and the overall socio-economic life in Kenya. While these benefits are important, showing creativity and entrepreneurship, there is a negative side to the matatu industry that we cannot deny. The matatu industry has been associated with violence, crime and insecurity, often leading to the sector being perceived negatively by the public. We are not necessarily saying that the matatu vehicle itself generates crime, violence and insecurity. Rather, the environment in and around the matatu industry is used by people to commit crime and cause insecurity.

This chapter examines crime, violence and safety in and around the matatu sector as a fare-paying-passenger transportation field in Kenya. First the chapter clarifies what constitutes crime, violence and safety, and how these concepts are utilized in and around the matatu sector. A delineation of these terms, and in particular how they are applied in this chapter is crucial to understanding what we mean when using technical concepts that are normally defined and associated with legal systems. The second section discusses and provides examples of crime, violence and safety in and around matatu as a fare-paying-passenger field in transportation. The types of crime, violence and safety discussed are crime and violence against passengers in general; crime and violence among touts, stage managers, drivers of matatu vehicles as a result of competing for passengers; matatu fare-related crime and violence; violence and crime against women and children (the 'weaker' in society); crime and violence as a result of overcrowding and speeding leading to road traffic collisions; 'state-legalized' crime and violence sanctioned and used by government and politicians for political gains; and injuries and fatalities associated with road traffic crashes. All these crimes, violence and injuries point to the need to examine values and ethics in transport service provision. If profit and greed dominate the matatu stakeholders or any transport activity, then this thinking and way of acting leads to less regard for passengers, who are affected by such issues as crime, violence, injuries, pollution and congestion. The transport industry, like other socio-economic sectors, provides a setting that can be used to promote conditions for improving quality of life for both human beings and the environment (Whitelegg 2013).

What do These Words Mean: Crime, Violence and Safety?

Violence

Violence is "the intentional use of physical force or power, threatened or actual, against oneself, another person, or against a group or community, that either results in or has a high likelihood of resulting in injury, death, psychological harm, maldevelopment, or deprivation" (Krug et al. 2002: 5). In this definition verbal abuse used to threaten someone and any other abuse which can cause trauma and psychological harm is included. In this chapter, all these forms of violence mentioned in the definition provided are considered.

Crime

According to the Collins English Dictionary and Thesaurus (2006:185), crime refers to offence, felony, misdeed and dishonesty. There are several other words used to describe crime. Generally, crime has two major meanings. In the first category are concepts such as offence, wrong, sin, misdeed, felony, fault, misdemeanour and transgression. In the second category are concepts related to corruption, wrongdoing, misconduct, law-breaking and delinquency. Looking further at the noun 'wrong', we get words like insult, injure, harm, wound, ill-treat, abuse, sin against and offence. Crime is therefore an all-embracing word. We may look at any behaviour that is experienced and defined as a wrongdoing against someone as a crime even if not all actions or deeds can necessarily be construed as breaking of laws for which some legal systems can ultimately prescribe a conviction. Defining and addressing crime has been central to management of human societies over the years. There are elaborate rules, procedures and institutions in virtually every society directed at crime prevention in an effort to ensure safety and security as people go about their business.

Road Safety

While safe movement of people and goods is a key concern in transport planning, road traffic collisions do occur, affecting not only traffic flow but also causing damage to human life, property and the environment. There are several words that are used: road traffic crashes, road traffic collisions, road traffic injuries and motor vehicle crashes. The use of the word "road traffic accidents" has been challenged as it is associated with looking at road traffic crashes as if they are inevitable and therefore not possible to be prevented. Despite this challenge, including a ban on the use of "accidents" in manuscripts submitted to the *British Medical Journal*, one still comes across the word accidents in contemporary journal papers, books and research reports. It would appear as if trying to change from the use of "accident" to "injury" or 'crash" is like fighting a strongly established habit. Nevertheless, our concern is with collisions involving different modes of transport using the road.

The matatu vehicle is one of the means of transport involved in road traffic crashes in Kenya. As several authors have pointed out, there are several factors leading to road traffic crashes and resulting consequences in Kenya (see for instance, Odero et al. 2003 and Nantulya and Muli-Musime 2001).

Contextualizing Crime, Violence and Safety Associated with the Matatu Sector

Violence and crime associated with the matatu sector takes many forms. We therefore examine specific types of violence and crime in order to understand their causes and effects.

Crime and Violence as a Result of Competing for Passengers and Controlling Them

An example of a commonly committed crime and violence used against innocent passengers is the rough and forceful way conductors, stage workers and even some matatu drivers handle passengers. As the prospective passengers approach a matatu stage, they are pushed and stopped by force. Those who have luggage have it pulled and forcefully taken away. Even before they recognize who has taken the luggage, other touts surround the passenger and finally those who succeed push the passenger and put her or him into a matatu. Sometimes passengers are pushed into a vehicle which is not of their choice. Other passengers, mostly women carrying luggage and maybe a child or two, lose their luggage and helplessly see their children pulled away from them. All this harassment and trauma that passengers have to endure gives a picture of violence and crime committed against passengers-to-be. This type of crime and violence is committed against many passengers in and around matatu stages and also along the road as matatu drivers, conductors and other workers aggressively look for passengers in order to fill up their vehicles. Force and abusive language are also used when the matatu crew squeezes passengers into the vehicles without sympathy. The touts (*manambas*) and conductors gain a position of authority and their behaviour can be described as that of lords of the matatus while passengers are turned into 'captive travellers' (Aduwo 1990). wa Mungai and Samper (2006: 58) state:

> As soon as they board a *matatu*, they are under the control of a *manamba*, who tells them where to sit or stand. The use of Kiswahili imperatives, such as '*kaa vizuri*' '*toka*', '*songa*', and the inevitable '*leta pesa*', shows the asymmetry of power relations inside a *matatu*. The tone of voice in which these orders are delivered leaves no doubt as to *manamba's* authority. *Manambas* often fill their *matatu* to overflowing, since more passengers mean more pay.

The Kiswahili words, '*kaa vizuri*', '*toka*', '*songa*', '*lete pesa*', are orders given to passengers, who are virtually captive travellers, to 'sit properly', 'get off', 'push', and 'bring the money', respectively. Along with these directives, passengers are verbally abused and force exerted as they are constantly physically pushed to add one more passenger, a trend that was common in all matatus with a similar *modus operandi*. One of the authors of this book travelled once in a matatu vehicle when the father's car broke down and they were forced to use a matatu since the private car had to be left at a garage. The father tried to resist the push and orders from the touts and conductors, but they shouted at him and said something like: 'You are a useless person. If you do not do as we say then you get out and buy your own car'. The father tried to say, 'My car has just broken down and we are taking a matatu because it is late in the evening', but they did not care. Such language meant to ridicule passengers was and is still very common. This anecdote reveals the assumption common among matatu owners and workers. They assume that most passengers are the poor and low class who do not own and/or cannot afford to own their own private cars. While in most of the high-income countries such as Sweden, people from all socio-economic classes tend to use public modes of transport such as trains, buses and even bicycles to work, the Kenyan elite are known to cling to their cars both for convenience and comfort but as well for demonstrating economic status. Owning a car is a symbol of economic success and status. Hence, the perception of passengers by matatu workers is in most cases correct. Many who use matatu vehicles in Kenya are normally lower middle to low class workers who do not own personal cars. Some might have a family car, which is normally used by the man of the family, who has bought the car, while the wife uses a matatu. wa Mungai and Samper (2006:59) tell further of how such abuse can accelerate to actual bodily harm to innocent passengers:

> When people board a *matatu,* they surrender all personal control; they are at the mercy of the *manamba.*[1] Violence is never far away in a *matatu,* and failure to do what the *manamba* says can result in literally being thrown out of the *matatu.* During casual conversation, a university professor reported having seen a passenger thrown out of a moving *matatu* and severely hurt. When a fellow passenger is in trouble with a *manamba,* others tend not to interfere. I. J. P. Loeffler, a Kenyan surgeon, who has had to deal with victims of crashes involving *matatu,* notes that passengers 'do not intervene, do not assert themselves – they'd rather just pray – because they fear the man at the helm and his henchmen'.

Passengers within, around and in matatu vehicles are not only bullied and harassed as they approach the matatus and sit in them, but are also abused and harassed when alighting. Though matatu owners and workers' livelihood depends on these passengers who pay fares, which sometimes are abruptly increased and

---

1   *Manamba* is a Kiswahili word, referring to the conductor and/or tout who oversees fare collection, passenger requests to board and alight, and general management of use of space in the matatu vehicle.

especially in the evenings (at times resulting in matatu fare-related crime and violence described and discussed in the next section), they unfortunately do not accord them the respect that they deserve. Violent exerted pushing, public shaming and humiliation and general discomfort were and still are common in the matatu industy. There has been, however, an increase in order and reduction in harassment since there are some matatus that still adhere to the 2003 Michuki rules, among which is the requirement for matatu vehicles to carry sitting passengers only.

Other forms of crime committed against passengers include lack of privacy and loud music causing disorientation in passengers as described in detail by wa Mungai and Samper (2006) and Mutongi 2006). Mutongi adds other perspectives by raising issues as to why passengers do not question the matatu behaviour and states that some passengers actually encourage matatu conductors to mistreat other passengers and even encourage them to break the law by stopping anywhere on the road as well as speeding. What all this shows is how entrenched this behaviour is in a society which has 'condoned abuse' and how difficult it is to change. Crime and violence against passengers is a day-to-day matatu business behaviour that is taken for granted, creating a culture of acceptance based on the logic of 'that is how matatus are'. This explains why this abusive behaviour is rarely reported and even if it is reported no action is taken against the offenders. This 'condoned abuse' allows continual social, economic, bodily, spiritual and mental violation of passengers. Though these crimes and violence seem to be tolerated by passengers around and in matatu vehicles, they are not acceptable. Passengers may tolerate them not because they want to but because they have no alternative way out. The intricate relationship between matatu owners, workers and law-enforcing agents, and even the support enjoyed by political leaders, assign passengers to positions of subordination.

Is This Fiction or Reality? Matatu Fare-related Crime and Violence

Though the matatu industry provides an important transport service, Kenyan newspapers often have stories of serious incidents of mistreatment in the matatu industry. For example, Obuya and Agoya (2013) highlighted an incident in Kawangware area, Nairobi where a woman was killed over a Sh10 fare dispute. Locals turned on the matatu and burnt it. The 23 year old woman had Sh20 that she intended to pay as her fare to the city centre but the tout told her that she had to pay Sh30. This prompted an argument before the tout reportedly shoved her out of the moving vehicle. She fell on the road and was run over by an oncoming matatu. The driver sped off leaving the vehicle that ran over her at the scene. The crowd that had gathered at the scene started protesting and set the mini-bus on fire.

In another incident, reported by Henry Nyarora in the Kenyan Daily Nation of 21 May 2013, a conductor threw a male passenger travelling to Kericho from his rural home in Manga district from a moving matatu after a disagreement over a 10-Kenyan shilling fare. The passenger was reported to have died straight away after hitting his head on the tarmac road. This incident confirms what Aduwo (1990), Mutongi (2006), wa Mungai and Samper (2006:59) and Graeff (2009) highlight about the matatu passengers' plight, being at the mercy of the matatu workers. As Graeff (2009) has pointed out, these incidents of matatu passengers being subjected to harassment have not been systematically analyzed but they are so regularly reported in newspapers and highlighted in personal stories that they cannot be ignored.

Unlike other cases where passengers are intimidated and silenced, passengers in the vehicle involved in this incident, perhaps because of the magnitude of the violence which instantly led to the death of a fellow passenger, are reported to have reacted strongly, confronting the conductor who fled and then demanding the driver take the vehicle to Nyamira Police Station to report the incident. There were over 120 comments on the website where this article was posted, with many bloggers seeking to get an answer as to what had happened (see box 7.1).

Box 7.1

Reaction to a matatu incident

That's horrible. There was another incident similar to this some 3 months ago in route 46. But we since moved on. Poleni (Sorry) good people. Just move on!

Set Fares and fare stages, make it part of the licence agreement, this is disgusting that a so called Public Service Vehicle is operated in this way.

Do away with all idlers at stages and bus parks ... let us have few civilized matatu crew

Next time, have the driver stop the vehicle and help the man out. Really, common sense should not be that difficult to apply.

Poor man! RIP! Kisii/Nyamira matatus are notorious for even worse, wonder who will save us from this uncivilized lot that poses as transport crews!

Hi, anyone knows what happened to the killer in the story reported earlier at http://www.nation.co.ke/News/W ... ? We need to put an end to this stupidity.

This is so unfortunate. I can't believe it, and where are these so called Matatu association bosses in Nairobi who only talk when traffic regulations are tightened. We need to have a Professional Institute of Public Service Drivers and Conductors (PIPSDC) where training and Continuous Professional Development will be part of the career. This unregulated industry is becoming too much. If we can regulate Accountants (through ICPAK) why not the PSV permit holders.

... and worse still, nobody in that mat (short form for matatu) had extra 10bob to pay for the poor man, PATHETIC

it's really not about ten bucks gal, it's about a conductor who was stupid enough to throw someone out of a moving mat coz of ten bob .... why wouldn't he stop the mat and ask him to alight? ... .

Where is the human heart?

Sad but the bereaved family should move on. Money at all cost will be our undoing.

The Michuki rules have been thrown out of the window. The public should stop complaining coz they encourage this touts and drivers harass them. Furthermore you will find passengers being overloaded and if you complain your fellow passengers tell you to buy your own car. But anyway this should not happen at this time and age rip my fellow passenger

This is brutality of the highest order.

Sad indeed and the second time it's happening after the Ugwaru one sometime back

Source: Obuya and Agoya (2013)

Some of the comments in Box 7.1 and others not included here tell of how most of the commentators are horrified and angry towards the matatu crew and what seems to be the Government's apathy. Some of the commentators are almost in disbelief that this really took place, whereas others are not shocked at all as they have read or heard about similar incidents. They tell of a ruthless and merciless matatu regime all over the country, a narrative supporting the fact that the killing of this man by a matatu conductor is not an isolated case. They also tell of a government that does not seem to move fast enough to reign in greed in society which has led to lack of empathy for fellow human beings. What matters is moneymaking at all cost. Violence of this nature does not only affect the dead passengers; the other passengers who are firsthand witnesses are also affected. How do these experiences affect them as human beings and as passengers who continue to use matatus? How do they deal with this trauma? As traumatized passengers, do they stop using matatus or are they continually traumatized whenever they plan the journeys and when in these vehicles? How empowered or disempowered do these experiences make them? We raise these questions as a way of expounding on the effects of these incidents. The next group that suffers the greatest loss and pain are the relatives and close family members. These families are violated when their loved ones lose their lives in an unexpected and senseless manner. Family members are also traumatized knowing that their loved ones died because they lacked 10 (0.11USD) or 20 (0.22USD) Kenyan shillings. In many cases, close family members depended on the dead person for their livelihood and this becomes a double loss of a loved one and the livelihood that he or she provided. The families also experience violence committed by the state or government when the culprits are never brought to justice. Society at large and especially the matatu users are also affected as the culture of impunity perpetuates the violence and the degradation of respect for human life. Preservation of human life is therefore degraded. If violence and crime persist, then the life of the matatu passengers is no longer considered or treated as sacred.

Crime and Violence against Women and Children: The 'weaker' in Society

In the preceding section, we highlighted examples of incidents of brutal matatu violence to men and women. However, matatu related crime and violence against women and children takes place in different forms inside matatu vehicles, in and around matatu stages and sometimes occurs in other places. The example of women carrying children and other luggage described in the preceding section shows the stressful situations women and children face from touts scrambling for passengers. For mothers and children, this can be a traumatizing experience if they are separated. From the authors' experiences and those interviewed they narrate how children are often heard crying and calling their mothers while the touts use children to make their mothers follow them. Even when and if the children reunited with the mother, the harassment continued as described above. Crying children were rudely told to shut up and their mothers were ridiculed with questions like: 'Mother why are you not comforting your child? Have you stolen somebody's child?' The matatu culture embedded in a wider culture of many years of oppression by the government had created a *habitus* with dispositions of misuse of power and disregard for human dignity. Authoritarian systems, including Kenya until 2002, create authoritarianism at all levels in society, where citizens are treated as objects and not as subjects.

    Women and girls were also verbally harassed and terrorized by matatu workers. As passengers, women and girls were treated as objects in a patriarchical society attracting comments from the male touts. Mutongi (2006:561) presented an example of a matatu conductor who made attempts to flirt with girls who enter the matatu as if the girls had no right to ward him off.

'Legalized' Crime and Violence Supported by those in Positions of Power?

This type of crime and violence takes place as a result of the support and encouragement by the state and others in positions of power for using economically marginalized population and especially young men as a means to an end. In other words, this kind of crime and violence is an expression of lawlessness and the exercise of power in a corrupt society. Kahl (1998: 86) argues that demographic and environmental stress can increase the level of grievances within societies, which in turn can provide ruling elites with incentives and opportunities to exploit these grievances to serve their own purposes. In the late 1980s and early 1990s, a period characterized by a struggle for political pluralism in Kenya, activists fighting for multiparty politics and other elites from the ruling party exploited the population working in the matatu industry and the matatu stage environs to commit crime and violence by creating instability in already precarious areas. As Mbugua and Samper (2006:58) note: 'The *matatu* is a closed environment, a place of vulnerability; it is public, crowded, and devoid of private space'.

KANU's aim to repress the opposition, for example, led to the banning of the Matatu Vehicle Owners Association (MVOA), and in order to gain favour from the matatu sector, President Moi, through a presidential directive sanctioned the carrying of standing passengers by matatu vehicles, against traffic laws, and allowed individual matatu owners to operate on any route (Khayesi 1999, Kinyanjui and Khayesi 2005). The presidential action broke the law and was a recipe for chaos. The presidential action indirectly legitimized or gave support to lawlessness as a way of thinking and acting in the matatus *modus operandi*. Unfortunately violence and crime also became an expression of the matatu-field-related *habitus*, a sentiment well-expressed by a Mungiki member interviewed by Rasmussen (2012) concerning corruption and violence in the matatu sector. Rasmussen describes how and what the member who was asked about the reputation of the matatu and the fact that Mungiki controls routes said:

> He went on to explain how *Mungiki* in their engagement with the matatu sector operate according to the system, not the law. Then he argued that this was a political problem reaching far beyond the matatu sector and referred to the widespread corruption and underhand deals said to characterise both politics and business in Kenya (Rasmussen 2012: 3).

Rasmussen writes further that the Mungiki member's description of Kenya is shared by a journalist Kwendo Opanga, who states that 'the matatu culture is indeed a true reflection of the Kenyan public indisciplined, arrogant and corrupt' (Rasmussen 2012:3).

Crime and Violence by Jobless Youth and others Lingering in the Matatu Stages

The matatu stages often attract unemployed and economically marginalized young people, and to a lesser extent other sections of society, older men, women and even children, who use matatu stages as arenas for making a livelihood. While some sell a range of items, others find heavily populated matatu stages in many urban areas in Kenya offer an opportunity to steal by discreetly pick-pocketing without causing any bodily harm. At times they may use force to snatch handbags and other items or tearing a handbag to be able to get the contents. But when they are seen by the crowd, on-the-spot justice is often executed on these pick-pockets, sometimes leading to their deaths. The tempting crowded matatu stages, though precarious, are seen by those economically marginalized as arenas of potential opportunity.

Road Safety

Road traffic crashes do not involve only the matatu mode of transport. In Kenya, over 3000 people are killed in road traffic crashes every year (Republic of Kenya 2008) due to deficiencies in the road network, vehicles, road users and traffic law enforcement systems (Nafukho 2001, Nafukho and Hinton 2003, Kayi 2007, Republic of Kenya 2008, Khayesi 2010, Ogendi et al. 2013). Some of the injured persons who survive are disabled and require long-term rehabilitation. The road users who are killed or injured include pedestrians, cyclists, passengers in various types of vehicles as well as those on boda boda (bicycle and motorcycle), drivers, conductors and sometimes those operating businesses next to the road. While the relevant statistics are helpful, for example, pedestrians constitute over 40% of people killed in road traffic crashes, it is important to contextualize the analytical categories generally used in transport and road safety research. The pedestrians, cyclists, passengers and drivers affected by road traffic crashes are essentially members of the community who left home to attend to their daily activities. However, their journeys were disrupted and not completed as planned because of a road traffic crash. Some of them were injured, some died, others had to cancel their plans and so many other disruptions occurred, affecting families, employers, the police and society at large. In our data collection on transport and road safety in Kenya, we have been told by respondents of many incidents where a family waited for a child or a parent to return home but never saw them alive again. We have been told of cases of where families learn from newspapers or receive a call from a friend informing them that a beloved one who left in the morning is no longer alive and is in a mortuary, following a road traffic crash. Road traffic collisions lead not only to loss of human life and property but also affect individuals, families, communities and the nation of Kenya economically, socially and psychologically.

Newspapers in Kenya regularly carry announcements of funerals and some of these deaths are due to road traffic crashes involving matatus and other modes of transport. These newspapers also have headlines and stories on road traffic crashes. The information presented in Table 8.1 is a sample from a review of newspapers to illustrate the losses that result from road traffic injuries in Kenya. The table needs to be looked at from the point of view of what the crashes mean to families and individuals in terms of loss of life, funeral costs, pain, social and economic losses. We should not just look at the people killed and affected as mere statistics or one of those things that happen anyway. These figures, whether a few tens or millions, represent human beings with an identity and a role in society. If we look at the impact of road traffic injuries, particularly the alteration they bring to the ordinary life of people going about their daily business, then it is important that necessary measures are taken to prevent such avoidable losses from occurring. The information in the newspapers may not be a 100 per cent accurate but it shows that newspapers are highlighting the problem of road traffic injuries.

Table 7.1   A sample of newspaper headlines on road traffic crashes in Kenya

Headline	Details	Source
Kenyan roads carnage spiralling out of control	Over 3,000 Kenyans have lost their lives on roads in 2013 and more victims were permanently paralyzed. Kenyan public transport vehicles drivers (PSV) have a knack of breaking traffic rules with abandon. The government has re-introduced Alco-blow to curb drunk driving among other measures to reduce deaths on our roads	http://news.ke.msn.com/features/kenyan-roads-carnage-spiralling-out-of-control
The Stark Reality of Kenya Road Carnage	Example of a crash that occurred at Ndii near Voi on the the Nairobi-Mombasa highway is given in which 12 people died and 15 were injured. The exact cause of the crash is known, in this case speeding and overtaking at the wrong time, but little action is taken to make an example of him to discourage rogue bus drivers from repeating the same mistake.	http://www.the-star.co.ke/news/article-118501/stark-reality-kenya-road-carnage
Road carnage in Kenya: Irresponsible drivers a major factor.	Close to 2,929 people died in road accidents between January and December, 2013. More than 80% of these accidents have been attributed to human error: recklessness, overspeeding and mostly DUI cases.	www.thepeople.co.ke/42740/road-carnage-far-claimed-2929
How corruption on Kenyan roads is causing loss of lives	Kenyan traffic policemen, in cahoots with matatu operators, engage in bribery which results in many unroadworthy vehicles being allowed to operate on Kenyan roads	www.jambonewspot.com/police-mint-millions-as-kenyans-die-on-roads
Curbing road carnage: Vetting for all driving schools	Government plans on vetting all driving schools in Kenya to ensure the quality of training drivers are given is up to standard.	www.citizennews.co.ke/ … /15603-driving-schools-to-be-vetted-in-2014

A revealing description of the impact of encounters with road traffic injuries is brought out by Nantulya and Muli-Musiime (1999: 3) as follows:

> Road traffic accidents pose a burden at different levels of society. This can occur at the level of the individual, household, community, health system and national economy. At the individual level, the burden may be in the form of loss of life, loss of job, income and livelihood and cost of health care. At the household level, accidents can cause untold grief due to the sudden loss of loved ones and loss of support, income security and livelihood. Prolonged treatment and rehabilitation of the victim can lead to high costs of health care with attendant impoverishment and loss of livelihood for the household. Poor people value life just like anybody else: they will sell their land and other belongings to secure health care. At the community level, there is grief for loss of able-bodied members. In addition, the health care costs – often involving voluntary contributions by community members – can be a strain on the community resources. Similarly, the absence of a strong national security system implies that support for the bereaved family has to be taken up by the existing traditional system of community support. This further drains community resources. The burden of road traffic accidents on the health system is indeterminate.

Kenya has a basic policy and operational framework for road safety action (Khayesi 2010). There is a new national agency responsible for transport and safety policy in Kenya and institutions such as the police, government ministries and non-governmental organizations responsible for a number of road safety activities. A long-term road safety programme was formulated at the beginning of the 1980s. The programme had goals and targets to be achieved in the implementation period, 1984–1993. Road safety legislation also exists and there are experts in different aspects of road safety and related issues.

It should, however, be noted that the setting of goals and targets should be accompanied by effective and sustained implementation of the road safety plan of action. This in essence means putting in place an effective institutional framework, necessary personnel and appropriate resources. These include equipment, funds and related support. Implementation of Legal Notice No.161 was an example of the practical steps that needed to be taken.

Generally speaking, the implementation of plans of action has been found wanting in Kenya. It is not only in road safety policy that Kenya has not fully implemented a basic operational framework to realize some tangible results. This state of affairs exists in other sectors such as economic development, industrialization, agriculture, energy and education. Kenya has several five-year development plans, national strategic plans and targeted programmes. Research and an examination of planning show that over the years, Kenya has put in place policies and regulations for national development and transformation, examples being the 1965 Sessional paper on African socialism and its application to planning in Kenya, the 1983 district focus for rural development strategy, the industrialization transformation strategy, the 2003–

2007 economic recovery strategy for wealth and employment creation and Vision 2030 (Odhiambo and Mitullah 2007, Government of the Republic of Kenya 2007, Government of Kenya 2003). There have also been targeted programmes such as the Lake Basin Development Authority, the Kerio Valley Development Authority, the Arid and Semi-Arid Lands Special Programme, the Youth Development Programme and the Jua Kali Programme. In short, Kenya is not short of key policy direction and blueprints for action but the main problem that has been identified is the lack of sustained implementation of existing policies and plans of action in many sectors (Alila 2001). Perhaps Kenya can learn a lesson from Pinchot and Pellman (1999: 17): 'Most people face a choice: either go to their graves with all their better ideas unfulfilled, or give up on 99 per cent of them and take the time to push one at a time through to completion'.

A vicious cycle seems to have evolved at the national level with respect to the problem of road injuries in Kenya. The cycle goes as follows; several persons perish in a tragic road traffic injury. Statements such as "no overloading, speed governors are to be installed, no loud music and no speeding warnings" are issued. Enforcement officers become more vigilant though not for long; then they compromise on all issued measures until another major crash occurs (see Figure 7.1). A more or less similar pattern is observed in national policy; a need for action is noted, consultations are held, policy guidance is provided, initial action is vigorous, a lull period sets in until the same or another issue is identified.

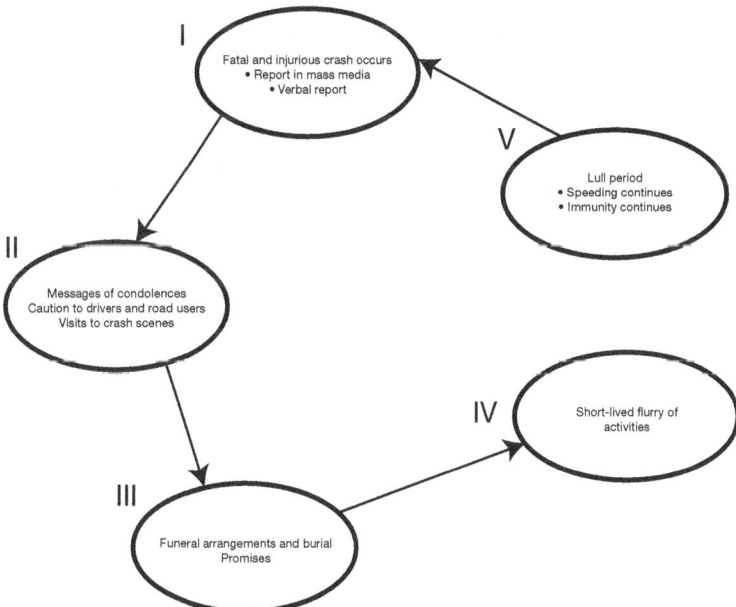

Figure 7.1   A generalised response to road traffic collisions in Kenya

In conclusion, and reinforcing the point made in Chapter 2, transport or the matatu service is not just about a vehicle moving from one place to another but more importantly about interactions among people in space and time. Whereas the matatu service facilitates this movement and there are many operators who are doing their best, there are some issues of violence, crime and safety like the ones illustrated in the preceding sections that need to be addressed by stakeholders involved in matatu entrepreneurship. There are basic ethical principles and issues like equity, sanctity of life, quality of life, inclusion, social justice and respect that need to be pursued not only in the broader area of human rights but also in specific areas such as transport infrastructure development and service provision (Whitelegg 2013, Lucas and Currie 2011, Schweitzer and Valenzuela 2004).

Summary

The following are the key points from this chapter:

- The matatu industry has been associated with violence and crime, often leading to the sector being perceived negatively by the public.
- The types of crime and violence found in the matatu sector include crime and violence against passengers; crime and violence among touts, stage managers and drivers of matatu vehicles as a result of struggling for passengers; violence and crime against women and children (the 'weaker' in society); crime and violence as a result of overcrowding and speeding leading to road traffic collisions; 'state-legalized' crime and violence sanctioned and used by government and politicians for political gains; and road traffic crashes.
- The crime and violence in the matatu partly reflects the crime and violence prevailing in broader Kenyan society.

Chapter 8

The Matatu Industry as Part of Entrepreneurial Efforts in Kenya

Introduction

One of the main pictures of Africa presented in the literature and the media is one of a continent in a crisis. While it cannot be denied that Africa faced and continues to experience a wide range of political, economic and social problems (see for instance Timberlake 1985 and Meredith 2005), some literature narrates the innovations and local creativity that have partly contributed to keeping body and soul together in Africa (Mahajan 2009, Radelet 2010 and Juma 2011). Entrepreneurship is one of the creative sectors that are highlighted as contributing to change in Africa (Kinyanjui 2012).

This chapter seeks to demonstrate that the matatu entrepreneurship belongs to a wider family of creativity and innovation in Kenya. Historically, Kenyan communities have taken local initiatives to look for solutions to the problems they face. There has been a creative response and an effort to develop some homegrown solutions by entrepreneurs in Kenya to address the environmental and socio-economic development issues facing their communities. Some of the services have filled gaps due to a decline in existing state service development. What is intriguing is the process of developing these services, some of which looked unrealistic and not viable but have grown to enhance socio-economic development. There are several examples of local solutions but we shall focus on a few to demonstrate diversity in the way the creative talent of individuals and communities in Kenya has been utilized. Our case studies will focus on Harambee, M-pesa, Solar Lantern, Iko Toilet, Adopt-a-Light Project, Ushahidi, Green Belt Movement, Marakwet traditional irrigation system and boda boda.

Harambee Spirit

The Kiswahili word 'Harambee' comes from a work cry (a a a a – mbeee!) meaning, ready – push (Hill 1975:1). The English translation is: 'let us work together' or 'let us pull together' and in Kenyan languages it means community cooperation or helping one another (Nafukho, 1994:42). In nearly all Kenyan communities, the term Harambee is a term or a cry for cooperation. It is a work song that is used to draw individuals together when they are lifting a log of wood, a roof onto a granary or pushing a car out of mud (Nyong'o 1981). It is supposed to be a purely voluntary and selfless activity (Nafukho 1994). In terms of development, Harambee means the pooling together of financial, human and material resources to develop a project such as a school, a health clinic or a bridge.

On the historical development of Harambee spirit, Nyong'o (1981) observed that it existed in Kenya even before the independence period. The African spirit that has existed in African societies since time immemorial, is grounded in cooperation and collaboration of individuals working together on agricultural farms, assisting each other in the building of huts in the villages, working together as a family or community to cultivate land, working together as a youth group to make bricks for commercial sale, as well as women and men working together removing weeds from the maize, yam, millet and cassava fields. In the case of Kenya, in the pre-independence period, even the colonialists used Harambee for their own benefit. For instance, Nyong'o observed that able-bodied young men left their villages in Nyanza to go and work on the tea estates owned by colonialists for meagre wages. When Kenya achieved political independence on 1 June 1963, Harambee acquired a new dimension and momentum and was highly encouraged by the nation's founding father Mzee Jomo Kenyatta. He advocated the logic of *uhuru na kazi*: that political independence had to go hand in hand with hard work which would lead to economic growth and development. During his swearing in ceremony, Jomo Kenyatta observed:

> As we participate in pomp and circumstance and as we merry at this time, remember this: we are relaxing before the toil that is to come. We must work harder to fight our enemies – ignorance, sickness and poverty. I therefore give you the call Harambee! Let us work hard together for our country Kenya (Mwiria 1986: 2)

From independence onwards, the Harambee spirit became very dynamic in the process of the country's development. Harambee from the founding father's slogan in 1963 led to the development of many projects such as the construction of schools later referred to as Harambee schools, health centres, cattle dips, access roads, bridges, the Harambee Institutes of Science and Technology, the Harambee Village Polytechnics, the Harambee Nyayo Wards, and the Harambee Technical Training Institutes. In addition, many students in need have been able to attend secondary schools and colleges through funds obtained from Harambee contributions. In 1991 when university fees were introduced for the first time in Kenyan public universities, a number of brilliant but poor students were able to attend the public universities through financial support obtained from Harambee events that were held all over the country. Within one year, over Kshs. 18 million was raised to assist university students in need (Nafukho 1994). Thus, Harambee significantly supplemented government effort in financing various development projects until 2002 when the newly elected National Rainbow Coalition (NARC) government initiated the Constituency Development Fund which replaced Harambee funding of constituency development projects.

In contemporary society, variations of the Harambee spirit are in evidence the world over, for example in the form of volunteering and service learning projects in the USA. For instance, the Association of American Universities recommends service learning as one example of high-impact learning activities that every undergraduate student should engage in before graduation. Even though Harambee functions conducted by politicians especially during election time were officially stopped and replaced with the Constituency Development Fund in 2002 by the then President of the Republic of Kenya, Mwai Kibaki, other informal communal ways of mobilizing resources in Kenya continued. In addition, churches, individuals and families still hold Harambee functions as a means of assisting each other in times of need. Thus raising funds to meet individual, family, institutional or community needs is grounded in the Harambee and African spirit of pulling together resources to assist one another. Harambee contributions include activities such as merry-go-rounds, parties, family welfare contributions, funeral contributions to assist the bereaved and mourning families, 'Sindikisa' women projects, and project-based fundraising activities held in villages and in urban areas among friends, family members, and relatives and organized in the form of *vyama* or social groups.

The *Vyama*, which are now wide spread all over present day Kenya, are deeply embedded in Kenyan culture. *Vyama* allow members to face investment opportunities, educational and training opportunities and challenges as part of a group instead of as an individual. The idea of *vyama* is quite different from Western societies. Unlike in the Kenyan community, where individuals count on family members and on many occasion, friends, when faced with problems and opportunities, in Western societies, individuals faced with a problem or opportunity usually rely on markets and formal financial institutions to address such problems and opportunities. *Vyama* are informal community organizations which are flexible in nature and built on social ties instead of formal legal structures. As the Kenyan economy becomes westernized, some *Vyama* are now registered as community-based organizations (CBOs) by central government and county governments (Nafukho et al. 2005). In case of *Vyama* that are entrepreneurial in nature, they get registered at the Attorney General's office as partnerships, societies or small business enterprises.

Kinyanjui (2010) noted that empirical evidence from Kenya's informal sector where the *Vyama* and matatus belong shows that the sector is not just chaotic or disorganized, as some of the literature suggests. It is pointed out that several factors such as retrenchment, poor economic performance, unemployment, and globalization can push people into the informal economy, but once there, they mobilize social relations and associations to fulfil multiple tasks and functions. In the case of *Vyama*, the social relations and ties are guided by the Harambee spirit, the norms, and values of the people belonging to a given 'Chama' (social group). Kinyanjui (2012) makes a strong case for the role of informal sector institutions in development theory and practice. In the book, Kinyanjui persuasively traces how ordinary people (*wananchi*) use non-mainstream mechanisms through *Vyama* to enable individual, group and community development which is guided by the Harambe spirit. It is pointed out in the book that *Vyama* are now considered socio-economic institutions of hope in

Kenya given the role that they play in realizing economic growth through wealth investments, individual and community development, social protection, and wealth creation and distribution. In this book, intriguing stories of how ordinary people in the Kenyan society use collective mechanisms for resource mobilization, investment, risk-taking and shared gains for the common good, guided and motivated by the Harambee spirit of *umoja ni nguvu* (unity is strength) is provided.

Wawire and Nafukho (2010) examined factors affecting the management of women groups' micro and small enterprises in Kakamega District (now Kakamega County). The enterprises started as informal social groups grounded in the Harambee spirit of pulling together time, effort, human and financial resources. In this study, it was established that the main objectives of the *Vyama* owned and operated by women included economic empowerment of women, promoting unity in the area, benevolent fund to assist members during times of need, encouraging family planning, spiritual support and uplifting religious beliefs of members. In terms of activities carried out by the women groups studied, majority were involved in animal rearing. Other activities included crop farming, trading, merry-go-round, embroidery, boutique, tailoring and craft, brick-making, pottery and fire cookers, tree nurseries, cattle dips, nursery schools, secretarial college ownership, grinding mill ownership, money lending to members and pharmaceutical stores. This long list shows that the transformative role of *Vyama* founded and operated by women based on strong social associations and ties are thriving and changing living conditions of the members. Box 8.1 provides an example of a financial self-help group.

Box 8.1

Ebony Micro Finance

Ebony micro finance is a Nakuru town-based self-help group that is very successful in its operation. Members of the social group are connected through social ties and association pulling together financial resources and providing loans to small scale traders, hawkers, retail shopkeepers, dairy farmers, poultry farmers, fish dealers, second hand clothes dealers, and hair salon operators. Ebony micro-finance serves traders who cannot meet conditions for loaning by banks and other formal financial institutions. While Ebony started as a chama (an informal social group), it is committed to serving its members and operates seven days a week in order to effectively serve them. The association now employees credit officers with technical expertise who work in the field by advising the members and evaluating the performance of the group members. While the operation of Ebony micro finance self-help group is now formal, what ties the members together is the Harambee spirit and the desire to see the small business enterprises owned by the members grow and expand in their business operations.

Source: Watoro (1999)

M-PESA

M-Pesa is an innovative mobile money transfer model that has eased financial transactions.

This is the story of entrepreneurial Kenyans using information and communication technologies to transfer money using mobile phones. Graham (2010) observed that when one thinks of the developing world, the last thing that springs to mind probably is not cutting edge technology. However, since early 2007, Kenya has been leading the way with an innovative mobile phone technology, the first of its kind in the world then, which has transformed the lives of millions of people and businesses. Hughes and Lonie (2007) noted that in March 2007, Kenya's largest mobile company, Safaricom, launched M-Pesa, an innovative money transfer service using mobile phones. 'Pesa' is a Swahili word for money while 'M' stands for mobile, hence the term M-Pesa. An entrepreneurial individual in the mobile company in Kenya saw an opportunity with the use of mobile phones, sought donor funding and launched a service where Kenyans could use mobile phones to conduct business and to send money (Nafukho and Muyia 2010).

The initial methods of using the post office to send money especially from urban to rural areas were very slow and unreliable. The commercial banks had become very selective in admitting customers and they also charged very high fees to their customers. Hughes and Lonie (2007) observed further that within the first month, over 20,000 customers were using the service, a number well ahead of targeted business plan. 'The product concept is very simple: an M-Pesa customer can use his or her mobile phone to move money quickly, securely, and across great distances, directly to another mobile phone user. The customer does not need to have a bank account, but registers with Safaricom for an M-PESA account' (Hughes and Lonie 2007: 1).

Ignacio and Radcliffe (2010) observed that services provided by M-Pesa had grown rapidly and served over 8 million customers then. This number has since continued to grow. In fact, the concept of M-Pesa which initially started in Kenya has now been replicated in Tanzania, Afghanistan, South Africa, India, and in many parts of the world. In the case of Kenya, just like the matatu concept, M-Pesa idea has transformed the Kenyan society by simplifying and facilitating trade, making it easier for people to pay for, and to receive payment for goods and services without having to make trips to commercial or cooperative banks. The benefits of M-PESA to the Kenyan society were highlighted by Jack and Suri (2010) in their paper entitled: *The Economics of M-PESA* as including but not limited to:

- Facilitates trade, making it easier for people to pay for, and to receive payment for goods and services;
- Electricity bills can be paid with a push of a few buttons instead of travelling to an often distant office with a fist full of cash and waiting in a long queue;
- Taxi drivers can operate more safely, without carrying large amounts of cash, when they are paid electronically;
- Consumers can quickly purchase cell phone credit (airtime) without moving;

- M-Pesa could increase net household savings by providing a safe storage mechanism;
- Facilitates inter-personal transactions, which could improve the allocation of savings across households and businesses by deepening the person-to-person credit market;
- Could increase the average return to capital, thereby producing a feedback to the level of saving;
- By making transfers across large distances trivially cheap, M-Pesa improves the investment in, and allocation of human capital as well as physical investment;
- Households may be more likely to send members to high-paying jobs in distant locations (e.g., the capital), either on a permanent or temporary basis, and to invest in skills that are likely to earn a return in such places but not necessarily at home;
- M-Pesa could affect the ability of individuals to share risk;
- By expanding the geographic reach of these networks, M-Pesa may allow more efficient risk sharing;
- M-Pesa facilitates timely transfer of small amounts of money. Instead of waiting for conditions to worsen to levels that cause long term damage, M-Pesa might enable support networks to address or manage short-term financial needs;
- M-Pesa allows households to spread risk. They may be led to make more efficient investment decisions, avoiding the trade off between risk and return that they would otherwise face.

Mwaniki (2013) reported that M-Pesa had grown to become the biggest bank in Kenya by customer deposits. Thus, the customers' cash held by mobile phone companies by December 2012 had reached Kshs. 226 billion (US$2.7 billion), making the telecoms firms Kenya's biggest bank in terms of deposits. In terms of growth, Kenya's four mobile firms, Airtel, Orange, Safaricom and Yu, increased by 10 per cent between October and December, 2012. Mwaniki noted further that the amount of money transacted by M-Pesa had surpassed the cash held by the country's biggest commercial bank, Kenya Commercial Bank, whose total deposit was Kshs. 223 billion for its local operations. Regarding the number of customers, the number of mobile money transfer subscribers grew by 9.4 per cent to 21.1 million up from 19.3 million as reported by the Communications Commission of Kenya. In terms of savings, Kariuki (2013) noted that mobile phone money services had become the preferred avenue of savings around sub-Saharan Africa. M-Pesa has therefore recorded tremendous growth and provides mobile money services for the people who were initially unbanked and were also never considered credible customers by commercial banks in Kenya.

The benefits and risks of M-Pesa are similar to those of the matatu; they both started small with a focus on poor people living in rural and unplanned urban areas and later spread to the entire country. They also have an informal nature of operation, and the services that they provide are efficient and flexible. Above all, both the matatu industry and M-Pesa have totally transformed society. Like the Grameen Bank in Bangladesh which was started for the poor, M-Pesa opened banking space, especially electronic money transactions, to many people that had initially been excluded by mainstream banking sector.

Solar Lantern

One of the positive things happening in Kenya is the rural electrification programme which aims at extending electricity supply to all schools, health centres, trading centres, markets and any public institution all over the nation. As a result, many rural households relying on wood fuel as the main source of energy for domestic needs are now able to access electric supply.

The solar lantern initiative represents an effort to address energy needs in both rural and urban areas of Kenya. This initiative is a compelling story of creativity by a talented boy born and raised in rural Kenya who turned a dream into reality (Bwisa and Nafukho 2012). Evans Wadongo, while growing up in rural areas with no electricity, used a kerosene lamp for studying but was able to pass national examinations and get admission into Jomo Kenyatta University of Agriculture and Technology (JKUAT) to pursue a Bachelor degree in Electronics and Computer Engineering. At the university, he had plenty of light and used electricity as the main source of energy for lighting. Evans did not however forget his experience in rural Kenya and always reflected on many children in the villages who were struggling with reading using dimly lit kerosene lamps like he did. He always dreamed of an innovation that could improve reading conditions for millions of children in rural communities similar to his home village.

While at university, Evans invented a solar lamp, the first of its kind in the world known as *Mwanga Bora* (a Kiswahili word for good light). His initial idea was to make just one solar lamp and take it to his own family. This one lamp was such a success story that led to a programme known as 'Use Solar, Save Lives'. By 2004, about 15,000 solar lamps had been produced and distributed to families in rural Kenya. It was anticipated that by 2015, about 100,000 solar lamps will have been manufactured. Evans has constituted a team for a project called 'Use Solar, Save Lives'. The team identifies impoverished communities that rely on kerosene lamps for lighting. They hand out lamps to the community members who are often a women's group, and encourage them to pool the money they would have used to buy the kerosene to start entrepreneurial activities.

Evans Wandongo's invention of solar lamps has been recognized in the following ways:

- Selected as a Cable National Network (CNN) Top Ten Hero for 2010;
- Was honoured at an All Star Tribute show in Hollywood by Oscar winning actress, Halle Berry;

- Winner for the inaugural 'Man who changed the world award' in honour of former Soviet Union president and Nobel winner, Mikhail Gorbachev, along with CNN founder Tedd Turner, Tim Berners-Lee and Robert Cailliau the inventors of the World Wide Web (WWW);
- Featured on CNN, BBC, AFP, France 24, MBC South Korea, K24 TV, NTV, Citizen TV, KBC TV, German Radio, KISS FM, Capital FM, Radio Jambo, Nation Newspaper, The Star newspaper, The People newspaper, Passion magazine, Parents magazine, Management magazine and several online news sources. His story is therefore in the public domain.

Iko Toilet

Urban basic services such as clean drinking water and public toilets are inadequate in most cities in Africa. Apart from inadequate housing, roads and water supply, basic services such as waste management, including provision and maintenance of toilets are poorly managed and maintained in African cities (Attoh 2010). Population growth in a city like Nairobi is not well matched with development or improvement of basic services. The population of Nairobi was estimated to be 3.1 million people in 2009 (Kenya Mpya 2014). The then local government and now the Nairobi County government has not met the demand for basic services for this growing population. More or less the same story of a growing population and lagging service provision is repeated in virtually all urban centres in Kenya.

There are people and groups that take initiative to complement the government in the development of urban basic services. An example of such an effort is the Iko Toilet solution that was developed by David Kuria, an architect by profession, who came up with an idea aimed at ensuring that trips to city toilets were both pleasant and memorable for the toilet users (Bwisa and Nafukho 2012). David dreamed of transforming the idea that city toilets were not all about filth as it had always been the case prior to his innovation. Concerned about lack of toilets in most towns and informal settlements in Kenya and focused on addressing the welfare of low-income people in the city, David quit a well-paying job as an architect with a non-governmental organization to engage in 'toilet' business. He designed an ecologically friendly toilet which he named 'Iko', a Kiswahili word meaning 'there is'. Therefore Iko toilet means there is a toilet for your use.

David designed and built an award-winning Iko toilet, a concept that envisions the idea of a 'toilet mall' where toilets are availed at the modest cost of Kshs 5 (USD 0.05) as well as shops that stock snacks and barber shops. Tapped music is also offered to the toilet users. David's innovation has been recognized world over and he has received the following awards:

- Guinness World Record 2010;
- UN Dubai International Best Practices Award 2010;
- Africa Social Enterprise of the Year 2009 by World Economic Forum;

- Ashoka Fellowship on Public Innovation for 2008;
- Lemelson Fellowship on technological innovations;
- World Toilet Organization Hall of Fame 2008;
- Schwab Fellowship on social entrepreneurship 2009;
- Citation by President Bill Clinton during the Clinton Global Initiative 2009.

Iko toilet is not the only initiative by a concerned Kenyan citizen to address a deficiency in urban services. Another example is the 'Adopt-a-Light' project. As indicated in Khayesi et al. (2010), provision and maintenance of street lights by the Nairobi City Council was problematic for a fairly long period of time until the 'Adopt-a-Light' Intervention or company, belonging to Esther Passaris, started to restore street lighting in 2002. As explained by UNISA Centre for Corporate Citizenship et al (2007), 'Adopt-a-Light' is a public–private partnership with the Nairobi City Council. The project is funded through revenue collection for outdoor advertising in the city and sponsor payments for adopting a light. The businesses that adopt a light get a return on investment by placing advertisements on the streetlight. Lack of street lights in the central business district and residential areas partly contributed to street crime as muggers easily operated under the cover of darkness.

Ushahidi Crowdmapping Platform for Justice and Accountability

As the wise sayings go, 'in every challenge, there is an opportunity hidden waiting to be exploited" and "necessity leads to invention', the violence related to the 2007 general elections in Kenya led to an innovative approach to searching for lost persons. In December 2007, Kenya held general elections and violence erupted when the incumbent Mwai Kibaki was declared the winner in the face of charges of vote rigging from the supporters of his main challenger, Raila Odinga. The violence quickly spread across ethnic lines in urban and rural areas far away from the reach of both the local and international media.

One of the problems that arose was searching for people who had lost contact with family members and friends. It was not easy for family members to tell whether these people were injured or killed or were still alive but not contactable. An innovative response to this problem came from a Kenyan lawyer, Ory Okolloh, technologists, and bloggers who quickly created software referred to as the Ushahidi Crowdmap. The word crowd referred to Kenyans across the country who were able to use the Ushahidi digital platform for justice and accountability using mobile phones, text messages and Google maps to convey what they were witnessing. Ushahidi is a Kiswahili word that means witnessing or testifying. The reports provided on the platform were then added onto an online map and within a few days, all those individual witnesses had together compiled a very touching picture of the violence that had occurred. The Guardian pointed out: '… Ushahidi was born after two sleep-deprived days of coding'.

From this Kenyan invention that was born out of necessity, Ushahidi Crowdmap has been adopted and is being used by people and communities faced with circumstances similar to what Kenyans faced after the 2007 general elections. Ushahidi Crowdmap software has been found to be better overall at reporting acts of violence as they happen. For instance, after the British Petroleum oil spill in the United States, a witness pollution map was used to report the impact of the spill. Those affected by the Middle East and North Africa uprisings and Japan's earthquake and tsunami events have all used an incident report system created by the Ushahidi Crowdmap in Kenya.

Green Belt Movement

Environmental degradation poses threats to the survival of humanity and sustainability of physical ecology. For example, in the case of Africa, climate change and desertification are the twin interlocking and most severe environmental problems hindering progress towards sustainable development in the region (Darkoh 2014). Climate change is contributing to reduced and unreliable rainfall, hotter temperatures and the spreading of diseases such as malaria, diarrhoea, cholera, dengue fever and meningitis, which cause death and suffering for thousands of people. While substantial information on what needs to be done to protect the environment and improve the quality of human life exists, the challenge is the translation of this knowledge into viable solutions at both the micro and macro levels. Innovative grassroots efforts have been explored to address the problem of existing unsustainable development. One such effort is the Green Belt Movement (GBM).

GBM is an environmental organization that supports communities, especially women, to conserve the environment and improve livelihoods. The movement was founded in 1977 by the late Wangari Maathai, a Nobel Peace Laureate. The vision of GBM is one of a value-driven society of people who consciously work for continued improvement of their livelihoods and a greener, cleaner world. Its mission is to strive for better environmental management, community empowerment, and livelihood improvement using tree-planting as an entry point. The values it promotes are love for environmental conservation; self and community empowerment; volunteerism; and accountability, transparency and honesty.

The Movement organized small groups of poor community members in both rural and urban settings to grow, plant, and care for trees in 'greenbelts' on public and private land. The Movement has organized more than 6,000 groups in poor villages and urban areas throughout Kenya and has planted over 20 million trees. Over the last 10 years, GBM has adopted a 'conscientization' approach to mobilize community consciousness for self-determination, equity, improved livelihoods, and environmental conservation. It has helped hundreds of grassroots leaders to advocate social, economic, and political justice. Internationally, GBM has begun to facilitate a Pan-African Network to assist 'green consciousness' and social justice groups in other African countries to develop similar approaches to community mobilization. GBM promotes grassroots mobilization, 'conscientization' and leadership development through environmental activities. It has facilitated the planting of 20 million trees in Kenya at a 70 per cent survival rate and mobilized 50,000 Kenyan households to care for the environment and improve their own welfare. Information about GBM is available at http://www.greenbeltmovement. org/who-we-are.

In addition to promoting the planting of trees, Wangari Maathai took personal initiatives, at personal risk, to challenge environmental destruction. The key and controversial ones are the Uhuru Park Construction Project, the Kenya Government Karura Forest Project, and her contribution to Democracy in Kenya.

The Uhuru Park Construction Project. Economists of education have correctly observed that the returns on investment in education can be of a pecuniary and non-pecuniary nature (Psacharopoulos 1985, Psacharopoulos 1994). In the case of non-pecuniary returns, one educated individual can help bring spillover benefits to many people in society. Wangari Maathai's campaign to stop the Kenyan government's project of constructing the tallest building in Africa in the heart of Nairobi is one classic example. In October 1989, the Kenya government came up with a grand plan to construct the 60-storey Kenya Times Media Trust Complex in Uhuru Park, in the heart of Nairobi. The complex was intended to house the headquarters of the then ruling party the Kenya African National Union (KANU), the Kenya Times newspaper, a trading centre, business offices, an auditorium, galleries, shopping malls, and parking space for 2000 cars. The plan also included a large statue of the then President Daniel Toroitich arap Moi. Professor Wangari Maathai, who was the first woman in Eastern and Southern Africa to earn a PhD degree in Biology and had a great interest in environmental conservation, opposed this plan on an environmental basis. Using the power of the pen, she wrote many letters of protest to, among others, the *Kenya Times*, the Office of the President, the Nairobi city commission, the provincial commissioner, the minister for environment and natural resources, the executive directors of UNEP and the Environment Liaison Centre International, the executive director of the United Nations Educational, Scientific and Cultural Organization (UNESCO), the Ministry of public works, and the permanent secretary in the department of international security and administration. In addition, she wrote to Sir John Johnson, the British high commissioner in Nairobi, urging him to intervene with Robert Maxwell, a major shareholder and financier of the grand project. Wangari questioned the logic of the construction of a tower in Uhuru Park, equated it to such a construction in Hyde Park or Central Park and argued that a project of this magnitude would not be tolerated in the United Kingdom (Maathai 2006). Thus, Wangari's ability to raise the level of consciousness among Kenyans in general, environmentalists, civic organizations, the Kenyan press, and policy makers in Kenya and the world over therefore led to the collapse of the project. This was achieved despite a financier for the project having been identified, the ground breaking ceremony having been conducted and the land at Uhuru Park having been fenced off.

The Kenyan government reacted with anger to Wangari Maathai and referred to the Grenn Belt Movement as a useless and fake organization without knowing that her efforts to plant trees would in the future earn her a Nobel Peace Prize. In fact some leaders pointed out that if Professor Wangari Maathai '... was so comfortable writing to Europeans, perhaps she should go live in Europe (Maathai 2006: 190–193). It is noted that despite the public opposition to the construction project at Uhuru Park and Maathai's opposition to the project, the government went ahead and started the construction of the 60-storey Kenya Times Media Trust Complex on 15 November 1989. Wangari Maathai took legal action and sought a court injunction to stop the construction but the case was thrown out by the High Court in Kenya. The then Kenyan president, His Excellency President Daniel Toroitich Arap Moi, in a speech celebrating the country's political independence from the British, remarked that for Wangari Maathai to be a proper woman in the African tradition, she needed to respect men and be quiet instead of opposing the construction project at Uhuru Park in Nairobi (Maathai 2006).

The Kenya Government Karura Forest Project. In 1998, the Kenya Government developed a plan to privatize large areas of public land in the Karura Forest on the outskirts of Nairobi. The plan also involved freely giving plots to the then government's political supporters. When the Kenyan public became aware of this deforestation plan, they were up in arms against the government plan. Wangari Maathai joined members of the public in staging protests on a continuous basis. In addition, she wrote letters to the government and the press arguing against the destruction of natural forests since it was endangering the environment. She put her awards into action by going with the Green Belt Movement to Karura Forest, planting trees and protesting the grabbing of public land and destruction of the forest and the entire ecosystem which was against her environmental sustainability efforts.

Maathai (2006) noted that on 8 January 1999, a group of protesters including Maathai herself, Green Belt members, six opposition Members of Parliament, journalists, international observers, and supporters returned to the forest to plant trees in protest. The entry to the forest was guarded by a large group of men. When she tried to plant a tree in an area that had been designated to be cleared for a golf course, the group was attacked. Many of the protesters were injured, including Maathai herself, the four members of parliament who had accompanied some of the journalists, and environmentalists from Germany. When she reported the attack to the police, they refused to return with her to the forest to arrest her attackers. However, the attack had been filmed by Maathai's supporters, and the event provoked international outrage. In her support, the students at the University of Nairobi staged violent public demonstrations in Nairobi from January until August 1999 when President Daniel Toroitich Arap Moi announced that allocation of public land had been banned (Maathai 2006).

In her book, *Unbowed*, Maathai (2006) noted that again in 2001, the Kenya government planned to take public forest land and give it to its supporters like initially intended in 1999. Wangari Maathai with the members of the public launched protests and while protesting the land-grabbing and collecting petition signatures, she was arrested on 7 March 2001. The international community and the Kenyan public protested at her arrest and she was released with no charges preferred at her. In July 2001, there were protests to commemorate the *Saba Saba Day*,[1] Maathai was again arrested while planting trees at Freedom Corner, Uhuru Park in Nairobi.

Contribution to Democracy in Kenya. In recognition of her work and contribution to humanity, the following awards and honours were bestowed on Prof. Wangari Maathai during her life time and posthumously:

• 1984: Right Livelihood Award
• 1986: Better World Society Award
• 1987: Global 500 Roll of Honour
• 1991: Goldman Environmental Prize
• 1991: The Hunger Project's Africa Prize for Leadership
• 1993: Edinburgh Medal (for Outstanding contribution to Humanity through Science)
• 1993: Jane Addams Leadership Award
• 1993: Benedictine College Offeramus Medal
• 1994: The Golden Ark Award
• 2001: The Juliet Hollister Award
• 2003: Global Environment Award, World Association of Non-Governmental Organizations
• 2004: Conservation Scientist Award from Columbia University
• 2004: J. Sterling Morton Award
• 2004: Petra Kelly Prize
• 2004: Sophie Prize
• 2004: Nobel Peace Prize
• 2006: Légion d'honneur
• 2006: Doctor of Public Service (honorary degree), University of Pittsburgh
• 2007: World Citizenship Award
• 2007: Livingstone Medal from Royal Scottish Geographical Society
• 2007: Indira Gandhi Prize
• 2007: Cross of the Order of St. Benedict
• 2008: The Elizabeth Blackwell Award from Hobart and William Smith Colleges

---

1 This day first occurred on 7 July 1990 when a mass rally calling for political reform was held in Nairobi. *Saba* is a Kiswahili word for seven. Seven thus refers to the date as well as July, which is the seventh month of the year.

- 2009: NAACP Image Award – Chairman's Award (with Al Gore)
- 2009: Grand Cordon of the Order of the Rising Sun of Japan
- 2011: The Nichols-Chancellor's Medal awarded by Vanderbilt University
- 2013: Doctor of Science (honorary degree), Syracuse University, New York
- 2013: Wangari Maathai Trees and Garden dedicated on the lawn of the University of Pittsburgh's Cathedral of Learning.

Source: Norwegian Nobel Committee (2004)

Among the many awards that Professor Maathai received, the most prestigious was the Nobel Peace Prize. She was awarded the 2004 Nobel Peace Prize for her contribution to sustainable development, democracy and peace. The Norwegian Nobel Committee in announcing the award noted as follows:

The Norwegian Nobel Committee has decided to award the Nobel Peace Prize for 2004 to Wangari Maathai for her contribution to sustainable development, democracy and peace. Peace on earth depends on our ability to secure our living environment. Maathai stands at the front of the fight to promote ecologically viable social, economic and cultural development in Kenya and in Africa. She has taken a holistic approach to sustainable development that embraces democracy, human rights and women's rights in particular. She thinks globally and acts locally. Maathai stood up courageously against the former oppressive regime in Kenya. Her unique forms of action have contributed to drawing attention to political oppression – nationally and internationally. She has served as inspiration for many in the fight for democratic rights and has especially encouraged women to better their situation. Maathai combines science, social commitment and active politics. More than simply protecting the existing environment, her strategy is to secure and strengthen the very basis for ecologically sustainable development. She founded the Green Belt Movement where, for nearly thirty years, she has mobilized poor women to plant 30 million trees. Her methods have been adopted by other countries as well. We are all witness to how deforestation and forest loss have led to desertification in Africa and threatened many other regions of the world – in Europe too. Protecting forests against desertification is a vital factor in the struggle to strengthen the living environment of our common Earth. Through education, family planning, nutrition and the fight against corruption, the Green Belt Movement has paved the way for development at grass-root level. We believe that Maathai is a strong voice speaking for the best forces in Africa to promote peace and good living conditions on that continent. Wangari Maathai will be the first woman from Africa to be honoured with the Nobel Peace Prize. She will also be the first African from the vast area between South Africa and Egypt to be awarded the prize. She represents an example and a source of inspiration for everyone in Africa fighting for sustainable development, democracy and peace. Source: Norwegian Nobel Committee (2004)

On learning that she had received the coveted award, she observed:

> ... The news hit me like a thunderbolt. How was I supposed to handle it? How did this happen? How did they find such a person as me? I could hardly believe it. It was clear now why the Norwegian ambassador had called. "I am being informed that I have won the Nobel Peace Prize", I announced to myself and those around me in the car with a smile as I pulled the cell phone away from my ear and reconnected with my fellow passengers. They knew it was not a joke because happiness was written all over my face. But at the same time, tears streamed from my eyes and onto my cheeks as I turned to them. They, too, were now smiling broadly, some cheering loudly and hugging me as if to both comfort and congratulate me, letting my tears fall on their shoulders and hiding my face from some of my staff, whom they felt shouldn't see me cry. But these were tears of great joy at an extraordinary moment! (Maathai 2006: 291–292).

Marakwet and Keiyo Traditional Irrigation System

The Marakwet, Keiyo and Pokot people of Kenya have developed small-scale indigenous irrigation systems (Khayesi 2001b). These communities live in the arid and semi-arid zones of the Rift Valley region of Kenya. They are part of the communities within the Kerio Valley Development Authority jurisdiction.

These communities developed a system of furrows to tap water from rivers and streams and direct it to farms and villages. The furrows are old and it has not been easy to establish the date this irrigation system was constructed (Kipkorir 1981). However, furrow irrigation has existed among these communities for a long period of time. This duration of time largely explains why the extensive furrow system is embedded in the social lives of these communities. The furrows traverse several kilometres over varying terrain. What is intriguing is the way these communities have devised a system of water distribution, furrow maintenance and settlement of water disputes that is well integrated into the local social and economic system. Clan elders play an important role in the management of the furrow irrigation system (Soper 1981). The point we are advancing here is the creative response of these communities through technology, a system of furrows and a structure for water management to tackle the problem of water constraint in their local environment.

Boda Boda

Kenya, like other African countries, has two complementary transport and interaction systems in rural areas: a) a national and international system of routes, nodes, edges and services; and b) a local system of routes and services that links households, communities, villages and small towns to each other as well as to the national and international system. A substantial amount of the traffic flow on the national and international transport system in Kenya starts off as short distance walking, cycling, driving and use of public transport on footpaths, tracks, roads and railways in rural areas (Alila et al. 2007). There is a diverse rural production and transport system: distance, purpose, mode, routes, people and objects moving and interacting (Khayesi 1993, 1995, Kinyanjui and Khayesi 2005, Alila et al. 2007, Kaira 1983). There is also a substantial amount of traffic and interaction that does not get onto the national and international transport system as it is mainly relevant to the functioning of the local rural production and distribution system. Beyond a main road or highway passing through rural areas in Kenya or other African countries is an intricate and intense transport and interaction system made of footpaths, tracks, rivers, boats, bicycles, carts, animals, cars, buses, trucks and head-loading (Figure 8.1). Generally, rural transport has received limited support from national transport planning in Kenya and several other African countries. Farmers are often not able to transport their agricutural produce to the market because of impassable roads during rainy seasons. Further, households face difficulties in reaching healthcare facilities because of the long distance to be covered, in addition to the costs of health care. Accessibility planning is yet to take a central place in both transport and service planning in Kenya.

Though efforts have been made over the years to improve rural transport infrastructure and services in Kenya, there are still several gaps. In response to the unmet transport demand, especially for a service for short distance and low volume goods, a passenger bicycle and motorcycle transport service, commonly referred to as boda boda has been developed to fill this gap in both rural and

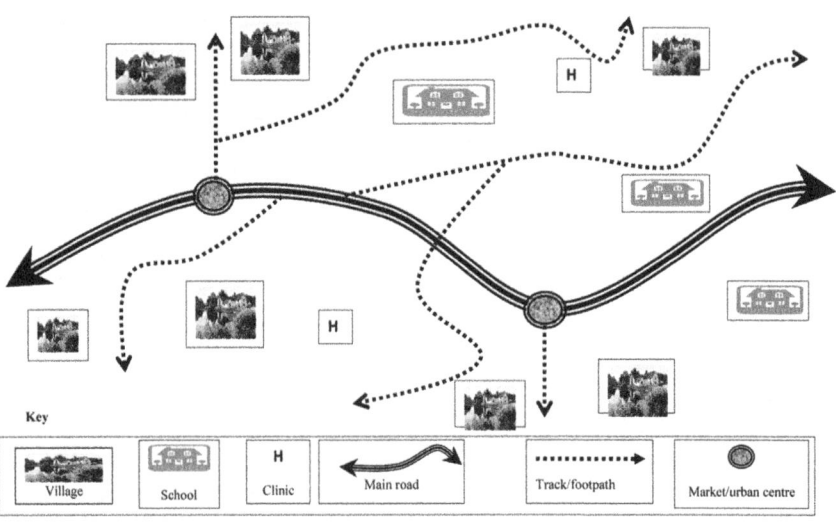

Figure 8.1   Rural production and transport system

urban areas in Kenya. For a long time, this passenger bicycle transport was mainly used in Uganda. However, in the late 1980s and early 1990s, it spread to Kenya. The growth and use of bicycles for passenger and goods transport in Kenya, especially in Western and Nyanza provinces, was rapid in the 1990s. In the 2000s, motorcycles started being used for this transport service. This form of transport is now widespread in Kenya, including Nairobi.

The physical requirements for operating boda boda make this business activity an exclusively young male undertaking (Alila et al. 2007). However it should be remembered that women are predominant when it comes to human porters, partly due to the greater, culturally-influenced role women play in the provision of labour for agricultural production and produce marketing. The main features of innovation of this service (Kinyanjui and Khayesi 2005, United Nations Development Programme 2005, Alila et al. 2007) are as follows:

- It has filled a transport demand gap with respect to short-distance travel and in areas that were not reached by the matatu. In view of the fact that some of the remote areas may be inaccessible to motorized transport, boda boda plays an increasingly indispensable linkage role between rural localities and the outside world. For example, those travelling to and from urban centres are picked up and taken right to their gates/doorstep and/or furnished with vital information regarding their travel route and the transport available.

- The operators have introduced a number of rules and procedures as well as organization into their operations. There are registration requirements, dress code (uniform), identification, operation from a specific location (stage) and membership of a credit and welfare association. This strategy is important for business as it results in trust between boda boda operators, the public and other small and micro enterprise operators who use this service. There are cases where business owners entrust boda boda operators to collect and deliver goods already paid for in wholesale shops or even giving them money for the purchase and delivery of the goods to their shops and kiosks. Thus, wholesalers and retailers are linked up and there is a possible reduction of costs to small rural entrepreneurs who often order stock in relatively small quantities. In both rural and urban areas, one can observe a clearly marked division of labour between motorized and non-motorized transport operators and also a distinction between large and small traders and passengers. For example, on a designated market day in rural areas, the merchandize, including maize, cabbages, beans, tomatoes and second-hand clothes arrive at the market in a pick-up or a lorry hired or owned by a large trader. The small traders then ferry small quantities to their kiosks/stalls using boda boda, handcarts, wheel barrows, human porters and boarding a matatu with the merchandize as personal luggage.

There are of course some challenges with this form of transport which include security, road traffic collisions and the working environment for the operators.

These challenges need to be seen partly in the context of transport, urban and regional planning. Despite an increase in bicycle and motorcycle taxis, planning has been slow in its response (Alila et al. 2007). The boda boda routes in rural areas are increasing while bicycle and motorcycle traffic in rural towns and even large urban centres continue to grow. In both rural and the urban areas, there is a policy failure to plan for bicycle routes and ensure safety standards are set and followed by motorcycle riders.

Summary

The key points from this chapter are as follows:

- The case studies presented in this chapter indicate that matatu entrepreneurship is not an isolated case but rather part of the creative response in Kenya.
- Examples of entrepreneurship and creativity in M-Pesa, solar lanterns, boda boda and the Green Belt Movement are transforming lives in rural and urban Kenya.
- The concepts of matatu, Solar lantern, Iko Toilet, Ushahidi Crowdmaping, Green Belt Movement and boda boda support Einstein's observation that imagination is more important than knowledge.

Chapter 9
Matatu Entrepreneurship as a Learning Experience

Introduction

Tuan (2011) has pointed out that professional planners, who have an urgent need to act, move too quickly to models and inventories, easily overlooking the rich experiential data that might have been collected. The pressure from society and sometimes from sponsors to produce results quickly can contribute to solutions being implemented before they have been fully tested or without room for further reflection and refinement as time passes (Greene 2012). Having presented the rich case study of matatu entrepreneurship in the preceding chapters, we use this chapter to reflect on two questions: (1) What lessons can we learn from the matatu entrepreneurship experience in Kenya? (2) What can Kenya do with the matatu entrepreneurship model that has developed and appears to be firmly established? We explore ways that policy and decision makers may utilize this innovative response to the gap in transport demand by providing an enabling environment for the informal sector, which is seen as critical to African economic development (Mahajan 2009, Moyo 2009). Profiles of selected African entrepreneurs have recently been compiled by Makura (2011), showing the importance of businesses in Africa's development. This book provides details about the experiences of such entrepreneurs as Mo Ibrahim of Sudan and Kwabena Adjei of Ghana, who have weathered several odds to become successful entrepreneurs.

Matatu Entrepreneurship and Learning

A major question often posed in history is whether humanity is able to draw any lessons from its experiences and use them to plan for the present and future. While there is substantial knowledge on past and contemporary human experience, the process of learning from it is not a simple matter of adopting or using this knowledge to address issues facing humanity. There are factors that either facilitate or hinder the application of this knowledge. It is therefore important to consider the issue of learning from matatu entrepreneurship in-depth. We draw on theories of learning to shed light on the possibility of learning from the matatu entrepreneurship experience.

There are several theories of learning but the management theories of organizational learning and the learning organization paradigm are most useful here to identify lessons from the origin, growth and the future development of matatu entrepreneurship in Kenya. Organizational learning refers to specific strategies and practices initiated by a particular organization, in this case the matatu industry, to promote learning among the people working in matatu related businesses (Nafukho et al. 2009). In the case of the matatu, these will include drivers, conductors, stage or route managers, practitioners, government officials and police officers, among others. Organizational learning as it applies to the matatu industry is a process which encompasses communication, sharing, and broad-based integration of new knowledge pertaining to the matatu into the matatu industry routines and systems (Bontis 2002, Crossan et al. 1999). Understanding organizational learning as it pertains to the matatu is essential due to employees' frequently having to adjust to police road blocks, route changes, passenger preferences, competition, government rules and regulations, police enforcement of traffic rules and municipal regulations. Organizational learning has been found to be necessary since it allows organizations to '... think proactively of using learning in an integrated way to support and catalyze growth for individual workers, teams, and other groups, entire organizations, and (at times) the institutions and communities with which they are linked' (Marsick and Watkins 1996: 3).

Human resource development practitioners and management experts recognize that learning has long-term benefits for the individual, organization, and society as a whole (Nafukho 2008, Nafukho et al. 2011, Ortenblad 2001). Learning should be considered as a decisive method for addressing most organizational problems. All individuals with an interest in the growth and performance of the matatu should utilize learning as a catalyst in understanding the nature and operation of the matatu industry.

The term learning organization, as opposed to organisational learning, refers to organizations '... where people continually expand their capacity to create the results they truly desire, where new and expansive patterns of thinking are nurtured, where collective aspiration is set free, and where people are continually learning to see the whole *together*' (Senge 1990: 3). The term *together* is critical to the operation of the matatu since it involves various stakeholders such as matatu owners, passengers, drivers, conductors, cartels, police officers, bankers, insurance companies and garage owners as was shown by the matatu tree in Chapter 3. The success of the matatu entrepreneurship is grounded in the ability of all individuals involved to relate and work together. Working together in the matatu industry is important to the organizational learning process and the learning organizations. In a complex and rapidly changing environment like the one matatus in Kenya find themselves in, only learning business entities that are flexible, adaptive and productive can thrive. This therefore explains the need for organizations to transform themselves into learning organizations. It has been observed: '... the rate at which individuals and organizations learn may become the only sustainable competitive advantage' (Stata, 1989: 64). Management experts agree that learning and the leverage of knowledge are the major determinants of success for organizations in the twenty-first century (Nafukho et al. 2009). Organizational learning is the key to adapting to a complex, rapidly changing and uncertain organizational climate that characterizes the matatu industry.

Matatu owners, drivers, cartels, stage managers, and route managers have learned out of necessity the importance of surviving and thriving in the matatu industry. Drivers for instance have developed the matatu language where they warn each other if police road blocks are ahead of them, if the road conditions are risky, if more passengers are ahead or if there are any dangers ahead. It is a *habitus* language that only those involved with the matatu industry understand. The language also changes very fast depending on the circumstances.

In an uncertain and rapidly changing environment like the one that characterizes the matatu industry, it is mainly learning organizations and individuals willing to learn, be flexible and adaptive who will thrive. Hence, the need for stakeholders in the matatu industry, especially those who are keen to develop a viable public transport service, to be willing to learn, unlearn, and relearn (Toffler 1970). To understand the matatu culture or logic of practice, it is important that the matatu industry is viewed as an organism affected by both internal factors within the transport industry and external factors from without the industry (see Chapter 1 on self-organization). Two main reasons can be advanced for why the matatu industry must transform itself into a learning organization. The first is survival which stresses that learning must be equal to, or greater than the environment change. The second is flexibility and superior service, which means that matatus must continuously strive for superior and quality service. We believe that the most appropriate strategy for the success of the matatu industry or any other industry is the learning organization paradigm which helps create curiosity and the desire for continued learning among all people in the industry. This in turn leads to creativity and innovation, which could be seen as the DNA of the matatu entrepreneurship in Kenya. In the next section, we go further to reflect on what policy makers may learn and do with the matatu entrepreneurship experience.

What can Kenya do with the Matatu Entrepreneurship Model?

The matatu entrepreneurship experience has been in existence for almost 60 years. It is now possible to identify and name its key features based on the information that has been presented on its development trajectory in the previous chapters. A model of the matatu entrepreneur's development path has recently been developed by Kioy (2011) (see Figure 9.1).

One can get into matatu business as an owner of a matatu or several matatus (Figure 9.2). As shown in Figure 9.2, level 1 is for entrepreneurs who do not have sufficient financial capital to purchase a vehicle. All they require is a bicycle. This is a very popular mode of transport in rural areas not served by matatus. The mode has also become popular in urban areas especially Busia and Kisumu towns. In rare cases, especially at the Kenya-Uganda border, some entrepreneurs who started with the bicycle have been successful to make enough profit to buy a matatu.

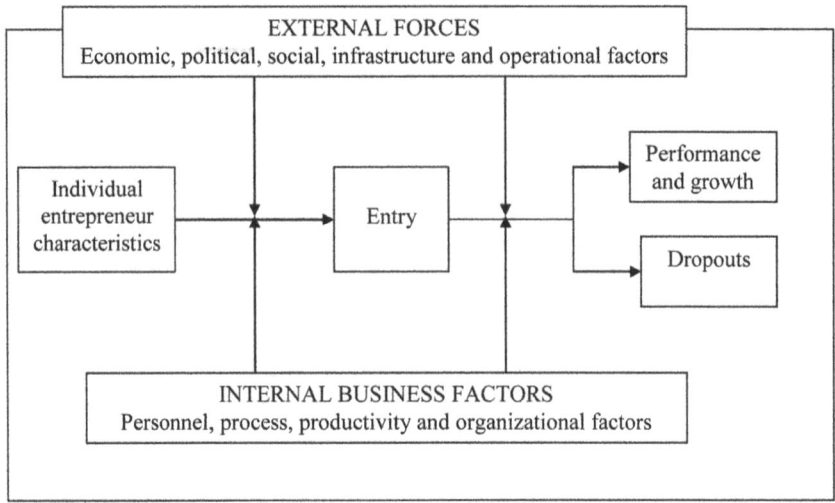

Figure 9.1   Matatu entrepreneur development path

Level 2 represents entrepreneurs who took loans or saved sufficient capital to purchase the box matatu (pick-ups that are built to carry people and goods). Level 3 consists of wealthy individuals who operate Nissans and Peugeot matatus. Level 4 entrepreneurs are *manyanga* owners (expensively built mini-buses that operate in Nairobi and other major towns) while Level 5 comprises of entrepreneurs with enough wealth to buy a bus or several buses. In short, the graduation levels in the matatu are intriguing: workers move from conductors to drivers and owners move from a single vehicle to many, and from having money to none or losses.

We acknowledge that the matatu industry started as an indigenous entrepreneurial activity but we also note that the existence of an elaborate self-organizing matatu industry in Kenya underscores the need for policy makers and the public to rethink the general perception sometimes presented of this sector as being chaotic and rowdy, and meaningfully engage with the structures, organization and participants in the sector. The sector and government need to implement programmes to improve the performance of the sector. There are concerns about how the workers handle passengers but there are no well developed programmes to address the underlying causes and offer job performance improvement skills to the workers. Such skill development programmes need to be offered not only to large transport enterprises such as airlines but also the small transport enterprises such as the urban informal public transport sector in East Africa as part of a comprehensive transport development programme (Nafukho and Hinton 2003). There are also concerns about the efficiency of the sector in serving the customers, especially with regard to time schedules, handling of passengers, and safety and pricing, which require a meaningful engagement among the different stakeholders with a view to finding viable solutions.

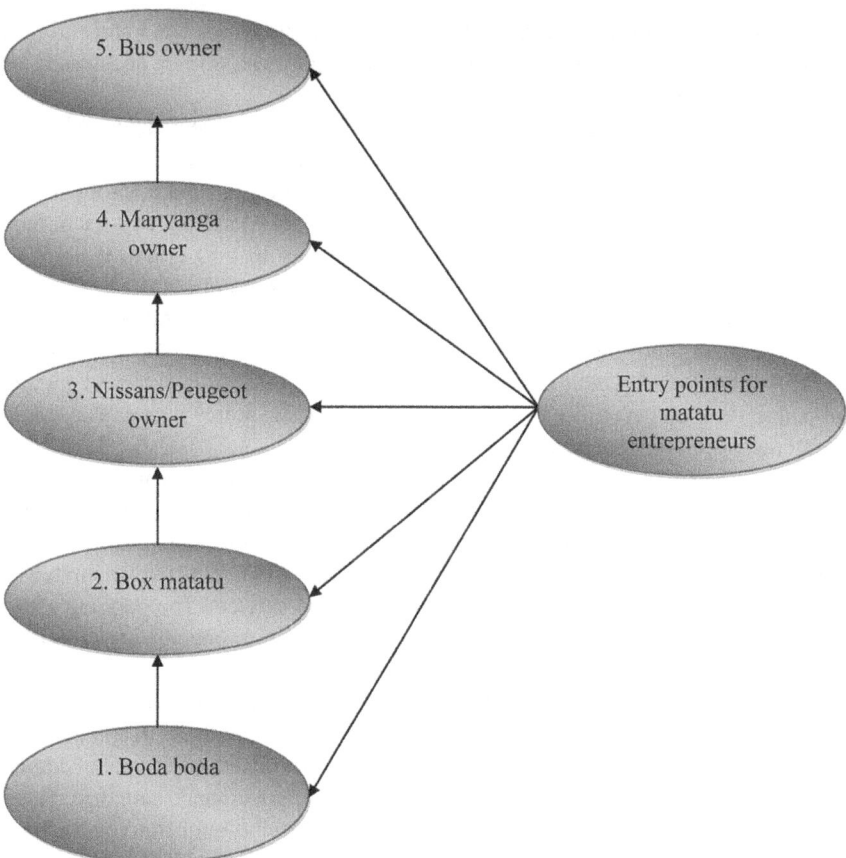

Figure 9.2   Entry points for matatu entrepreneurs in the transport sector in Kenya

As explained by Easterly (2006), there are two basic approaches that can be used in developing solutions to issues that face developing countries. The first approach is to follow the conventional planning approach which has blueprints for what needs to be done. These blueprints tend to be applied to situations in a top-down manner, reflecting the commonly used stage policy model that assumes linear progression from generating knowledge, implementing and evaluating it. This approach gives prominence to the role of planners, who are essentially prescribers of solutions to human problems. The second approach is to go out and search for what works, learn about the reality and adapt the solution to the local context. This approach places emphasis on active learning and searching for solutions from existing efforts. It looks at planning as an iterative process that is cyclic and dynamic, allowing for multiple sources and agents of change at any time and in any place. This approach helps searchers to explore new ways and embrace surprise, contradictions and uncertainty as opportunities and not necessarily as indicators of failure.

If transport policy makers and practitioners adopt the planner's approach, then they are likely to ignore the matatu industry and impose transport solutions from above. They will prescribe solutions to fix or even get rid of the 'problematic' matatu industry. However, if they adopt the researchers' learning approach, then they will embrace the entrepreneurial spirit in order to find practical ways of supporting transport entrepreneurship opportunities. It is not so much that they need to support the matatu in its present form but rather explore or tap into the logic of local transport business ownership and service provision to see how to develop a comprehensive and viable public transport service. Has matatu entrepreneurship helped to develop capability or generated issues that the policy makers can use in planning for public transport in Kenya?

The current Kenyan transport policy and the vision of an efficient and modern transport system for Kenya cannot be realized without involving the matatu industry and other stakeholders. Cities like Nairobi are planning for a world class transport system, including creating a bus rapid transit system. Will matatus be integrated as feeders or will they be left to run a parallel transport service? The ongoing effort and controversy about phasing-out the 14-seater passenger matatu vehicle offers a learning opportunity for decision-makers and matatu entrepreneurs to engage in dialogue and joint planning not only for the matatu industry but also for the transport system of Kenya. As already discussed, Kenya in 2010 adopted a new constitution that allows for devolved governance. The general elections of March 2013 brought into existence both national and county governance structure. There are now 47 counties, each with a governor and a local administrative structure, including a county cabinet. In 2013, a new transport agency, the National Transport and Safety Agency that was meant to bring together functions that were previously spread across ministries was created. These developments show efforts at improving the overall political administration and transport policy planning. They represent opportunities for dialogue and further action on the matatu entrepreneurship as part of the public transport heritage of Kenya. We do hope that this opportunity will be utilized by the public and policy makers to rethink the general perception often presented of matatu entrepreneurship as being chaotic and rowdy, and meaningfully engage with the structures, organization and participants in the sector in order to improve the performance of this sector in serving the customers.

There are a number of concerns about the efficiency of the sector in serving the customers, especially with regard to time schedules, handling of passengers, conditions of work for drivers and conductors, as well as safety and pricing, which require a meaningful engagement among the different stakeholders with a view to finding viable solutions. These issues require meaningful solutions to be developed and implemented by owners, operators, government and other stakeholders in the matatu tree that was presented in Chapter 4. There are regulations, policies and standards in transport and general public life that can guide the operation of the matatu industry. These changes will not occur by themselves. They require dedication and sustained input from all those who take shelter in the matatu tree. Evidence that a sustained effort is possible has already been presented in Chapter 4 with respect to the renewed effort of enforcing traffic rules in 2003. Corruption has been cited as a problem not only in the transport industry but also in other public affairs in developing countries. The zero tolerance to corruption policy the Kenyan government adopted in 2003 shows that this problem can be addressed. The ongoing effort of tackling corruption in the matatu industry through the 'Kitu Kidogo Out Project' shows that dedicated engagement can improve the quality of matatu and general public transport services in Kenya (see Box 9.1).

Box 9.1

Kitu Kidogo Out Project

The Kitu Kidogo Out Project was jointly operated by the Matatu Welfare Association and the Matatu Drivers and Conductors Welfare Association, and funded by the United States Agency for International Development from 1 November 2010 to 31 October 2011. Kitu kidogo is a Kiswahili phrase literally referring to 'something small' though it has connotatively carried the loose meaning of a bribe. Bribery of police officers by matatu drivers and conductors is widespread on Kenyan roads. The objectives of the project were to:

- reduce corruption in the public transport sector by 20 per cent by October 2011. This was to be achieved through anti-corruption training workshops for matatu operators affiliated to Matatu Welfare Association and the Matatu Drivers and Conductors Welfare Association. At the time of the launch of the project, it was estimasted that the matatu industry lost revenue in excess of Kshs. 1.18 bilion every year.
- improve the image of the Kenyan public transport sector. The matatu industry has generally been associated with disorganization, recklessness and general lawlessness. Through the Kitu Kidogo Out Project, the Matatu Welfare Association and the Matatu Drivers and Conductors Welfare Association sought to redeem the image of the matatu industry in Kenya. This was to be achieved through the adoption and enforcement of a code of conduct for all Matatu Welfare Association and Matatu Drivers and Conductors Welfare Association-affiliated matatu vehicles.

The joint secretariat of the project also hoped to form an active and vocal civil society mandated to champion the cause of the matatu industry in Kenya. We did not find a study evaluating the impact of this project.

Source: Matatu Welfare Association (2014)

How Has it Been Done Elsewhere?

We are of the view that there are several pathways to explore but they need to be worked out contextually. We wish to share experiences from other settings on how the matatu entrepreneurship has been or is being worked out in transport and national planning. We also provide an example of planning for overall transport system. We share these experiences given the practice we have observed in Kenya that political leaders and administrators often organize study tours to other countries to learn about planning so as to apply some of these principles when they get back home. The examples presented below may not be able to replace face-to-face learning experiences but they offer basic ideas and strategies that have been used in other countries to plan for transport.

The first example is from the city of Curitiba in Brazil. Curitiba, with a population of 1.9 million people and land size of 430 km^2, has a mode share of all trip purposes consisting of 45% of travel by mass transit (bus and train), 28% by private transport, 21% by walking, 5% by cycling and 1% by other modes (Journeys 2011). The planning experience leading to this travel behaviour is summarized in Khayesi et al. (2010), drawing on a study reported in detail in Ardila-Gómez (2004) and other studies.

The key points from these studies are as follows (Khayesi et al. 2010, Ardila-Gómez 2004). In 1936, the city of Curitiba authorized private entrepreneurs to operate bus services even on lines that competed directly with the tramways and the existing bus system. There were also many informal operators who competed with each other for the passenger market. Ney Braga was elected and became the mayor of Curitiba in 1954. He sought to address concerns and demands from the public concerning the quality of the bus service in the city. At the same time, the bus operators asked for a revision of the fare system as well as legal assurance of the security of their bus concessions granted by the city authority. Braga set up a commission to study the problem. The commission recommended the creation of exclusive or 'selective' areas to be operated by one or two bus companies. In addition, the commission recommended that the operators organize themselves into companies or cooperatives. There was extensive negotiation between the bus operators and the city government, which reached a consensus on these two options towards the end of 1955. The bus service was organized by zone of operation and run by 13 bus companies. This action improved the quality of service and gave the city government the ability to determine fares, plan services and determine schedules. The reforms initiated worked well for both the bus operators' interests and the city government, but after Braga left office in 1958, these interests diverged and there was conflict. Exclusive bus company areas and bus concessions have remained key features of public transport planning in Curitiba and other cities in Brazil.

The second example is from an ongoing effort to integrate the mini-bus or taxi industry in South Africa into the planning of the new bus rapid transit systems that are being introduced there. While the mini-bus industry of South Africa plays an important role in public transport, its historical origin in the Apartheid era and subsequent development within the political economy of capital accumulation has meant that it has deeply entrenched political and economic interests (Khosa 1991, 1993, 1995, 1997). Its integration into the new bus rapid transit system requires a deeper engagement to deal with all the diverse interests involved. While introducing the new bus rapid transit systems is a national effort, as would be expected, progress is not the same in all the parts of South Africa. In fact the bus rapid transit systems have been introduced mainly in Johannesburg and Cape Town (Schalekamp and Behrens 2013). A detailed case study of engaging the paratransit transport system in Cape Town has been prepared by Schalekamp and Behrens. We shall therefore draw on this study to show the way one city in Africa has decided to engage and integrate paratransit transport into a new mass transit system.

With about 6,400 owners and an estimated 7,500 licensed paratransit vehicles operating on 565 routes in Cape Town as well as a complex ownership structure, the local government decided to engage or hold discussions with about 100 umbrella associations rather than individual operators (Schalekamp and Behrens 2013). There are several issues that necessitated this engagement. Specifically, this included; (a) managing competition between paratransit and bus rapid transit system on affected routes, and (b) determining a locally appropriate mechanism to implement a national phased-out programme of bus rapid transit systems (implying phasing out mini bus-taxis from land transport). The first new trunk and feeder lines for the bus rapid transit system, locally known as MyCiti, opened in May 2011 (Schalekamp and Behrens 2013). So far, the outcome from this engagement has been developing contracts between the municipality and three companies owned by paratransit associations and/or formal bus companies. The three companies in question will have shares in MyCiTi and secure financial benefits or compensation for members who will have withdrawn their vehicles from the bus rapid transit route. The process is still going on, and Schalekamp and Behrens (2012) point out that the operating contracts are yet to be finalized and there are also emerging issues with respect to the method used to get the views of paratransit operators (relying on the views of officials of associations instead of conducting a survey), profitability of the new arrangement, and the disjuncture between national policy and local circumstances. This experience may provide valuable lessons as it is rolled out. We do hope that researchers will follow its implementation and dig deep into the process and outcomes and share their findings with other cities in Africa that are introducing bus rapid transit systems.

The third example is also from an ongoing effort of planning and developing a bus rapid transit service, this time in Dar es Salaam in Tanzania. Dar es Salaam has had to take into account the role of dala dala in the overall public transport system in the city. Kinyanjui and Khayesi (2005) show that informal public transport, locally known as dala dala, initially started in Dar es Salaam as an illegal transport service in response to a transport crisis. Like the matatu vehicle in Kenya, political intervention and support was critical in entrenching the role of dala dala as an important public transport service vehicle in Tanzania. A public transport company

118 Informal Public Transport in Practice

dominated transport service in Dar es Salaam at the time dala dala emerged in the late 1970s and early 1980s. This should be understood in the context of the national development policy and strategy in place at the time. Tanzania pursued a highly state interventionist approach following the Arusha Declaration of 1967. This involved, among other things, the nationalization of private businesses. This then explains why the Dar es Salaam Motor Transport Company, a British private company that had operated under a monopoly regime since 1947 was nationalized in 1970 (Rizzo 2002). After nationalization, two regimes were identified in the development of the market for public transport services in Dar es Salaam; near monopoly by the state provision up to mid-1980s, and *de facto* liberalization thereafter (Howe and Bryceson 2000). During the period of monopoly by the state, transport services in Dar es Salaam were provided by the *Shirika la Usafiri Dar es Salaam*[1] (Rizzo 2002). However, Tanzania experienced financial difficulties in the 1970s and 1980s, making it difficult for the government to provide funds to the nationalized transport company. As a result, the performance of the company declined steadily as reflected in the drop in the number of buses from 257 in 1975 to only 12 in 1998 (Rizzo 2002). Lack of foreign exchange and a generally harsh economic situation made the running of the public bus service grind almost to a halt.

The government of Tanzania responded in two ways to the transport crisis that faced Dar es Salaam. The first was to allow all ministries, government departments and parastatals to use their buses as commercial public passenger buses. However, this option did not adequately satisfy the growing demand for transport. The second response was to give official consent for private buses to operate, initially under the control of a government-appointed committee which registered the private buses. This move taken in 1983, allowing what had started as an illegal transport activity[2] in the 1970s to be part of the solution to the transport crisis, opened the door for dala dala to grow further. In short, the government intervened in the transport crisis by permitting any means of transport available to be used to move people, and one of the social groups that was greatly affected were school children. As was the case with the matatu industry in Kenya, dala dala received official and political recognition as the government frantically sought solutions to a transport crisis experienced in Dar es Salaam in the early 1980s. Since then, dala dalas have grown steadily and are presently a key feature of public transport in almost all municipalities throughout Tanzania (Howe and Bryceson 2000).

Dala dala service has been described as the backbone of the public transport service for the majority of the 4 million people who live in Dar es Salaam

---

1   This company provided transport services in Dar es Salaam and *the Kampuni ya Mabasi ya Taifa* (KAMATA) serviced inter-regional routes. This specialization followed the nationalization of Dar es Salaam Motor Transport Company.

2   When the private commuter buses emerged in the 1970s, they were perceived as illegal. Passengers used to pay for fare using a 5-shilling coin. Dala dala is thought to have originated as a reference to this coin.

(Schalekamp et al.2012). Despite this role, dala dala service has not been able to provide an efficient service. In addition to unreliable time schedules and geographical coverage, there are other problems facing this service and transport in general in Dar es Salaam. These include; inadequate infrastructure, pollution, safety and overcrowding (Institute for Transport and Development Policy 2005, Kanyama and Cars 2009). A solution that the Government of Tanzania and the city of Dar es Salaam is adopting to address transport demand in the city is to develop a bus rapid transit system. This is a long-term programme that will be implemented in phases. Planning for the first phase has been going on for over five years. A 20.9 kilometre bus rapid transit corridor has been designed and construction is underway. As is the case with Cape Town, dala dala operators are being urged to form consortia and bid for one of the two operating contracts for trunk and feeder service, or form a company in assocaition with an international bidder (Schalekamp et al. 2012).

The fourth example is Singapore's sustainable transport strategy. Singapore is a small island and it may not easily be compared to Kenya with regard to population and land size. However, the point we wish to illustrate is the exploitation of natural and human capital to develop a viable transport system. The long-term planning and implementation strategies for sustainable transport has generated a mode share of all trip purposes consisting of 44 per cent of travel by public or mass transport (bus and train), 33 per cent by private car, 22 per cent by walking and 1 per cent by cycling on this island of 5 million people living on 710 km^2 (Journeys 2011).

Singapore became independent in 1965. Like many newly independent countries, it embarked on a national development programme, with an emphasis on industrialization, focusing on export manufacturing and multinational investment (Cervero 1998, May 2004, Lam and Toan 2006, Khayesi et al. 2012). What is intriguing is not so much that the country had abundant resources but rather how the political leadership made good use of Singapore's primary assets; its natural port, strategic location and abundance of cheap labour. Like several newly independent countries, Singapore devoted effort to physical development and planning. The residential, commercial, industrial and recreational land use plan was not only prepared but also implemented.

Singapore began to experience rapid economic growth and the need for comprehensive planning was noted. This explains why in 1971, a concept plan (Ring Plan) was approved by the government for high-density housing, industrial sites and urban centres to be developed in a ring around the urban core, linked together by a high-capacity and efficient transportation network (mass rapid transit). A notable feature of planning in Singapore is that the Ring Plan guided Singapore's physical development for over 20 years. With regard to transport investment, it has been noted that it was guided by settlement and/or land use planning.

Singapore did experience conflict among different modes of transport which included human and horse-drawn modes, Chinese-run buses and other motorized transport as it prospered in the 1970s-1990s. The government moved in to consolidate bus services and banned slow-moving vehicles. The Chinese bus services were merged into three and eventually into a single state-controlled enterprise. Construction of mass rapid transport started in 1983. Many cross-island bus routes were replaced by a metro system by 1990, complemented by feeder and mainline bus services, a downtown shuttle system and a large taxi fleet. Generally, Singapore has implemented restraints on automobiles since 1972. These restrictions include taxation, road user charges, a vehicle quota system, an area licensing scheme (restricted zone) and electronic road pricing (Lam and Toan, 2006; Han 2010).

While some cities like Zurich have planned for transport under a decentralized political system, Singapore evolved a highly centralized strategic planning process under one-party rule which is thought to have provided unity, stability and the environment to implement the Ring Plan. Top-down decision making expedited the execution of the plan and the public ownership of land was also an important factor. A 1966 Land Acquisition Act empowered the state to take land for any public purpose. We are not advocating centralized planning but we are pointing out that different planning approaches have been used to develop sustainable transport systems around the world. While different political contexts may either facilitate or hinder the development of viable transport systems, it appears that a coalition of actors do play a role in either seizing the opportunities or overcoming the barriers in any given context over time.

Summary

The key points of this chapter are as follows:

- Features of the matatu entrepreneurship model are identifiable.
- The questions that arise are: What does Kenya do with the experience of matatu entrepreneurship? Can Kenya learn from this entire experience and imagine an alternative future which includes a sustainable public transport system?
- These questions are considered further in the final chapter.

Chapter 10
Matatu Entrepreneurship: So What?

Introduction

Two questions that a researcher faces as she concludes a piece of writing are: a) What is all the information that I have presented about? b) Where do I go from here? These questions point to the importance of not only presenting information but distilling it to determine the value it adds to research and practice. Thinking about the value of a study takes us to four further questions that a researcher has to consider in preparing a report or a paper. These are: (a) What did I set out to do? b) What did I do? (c) What did I find out? (d) So what? The preceding nine chapters have answered the first three questions. The question that remains is the fourth one: 'so what?' This question generally tends to be addressed in most studies by examining the findings in relation to other studies, and also providing recommendations on policy action and further research. We have already shown in part how this book relates to existing studies by outlining the four main points of departure for this book in Chapter 2. This chapter explores the 'so what' question further by looking at what Kenya may consider doing with the matatu entrepreneurship model.

Should Kenya Wait for *Godot*?[1]

The findings in this book show that the self-organizing matatu entrepreneurship has both positive and negative aspects. While it creates employment and provides a vital transport service, there are issues of long working hours, violence and security, poor handling of passengers, lack of respect for passengers, lack of professionalism amongst matatu workers, and road safety. Questions that arise from this include the following: How can the matatu industry be made to serve the public better? Should the matatu mode of transport be sustained or replaced by a bus system? How can the negative aspects associated with the matatu industry be eliminated or minimized? Who should take responsibility for addressing both the positive and the negative aspects of the matatu industry?

We do not wish to be prescriptive by giving recommendations which are too specific or suggesting one or two pathways as is often done in a number of reports

---

1   The phrase 'wait for Godot' is taken from a play by Samuel Becket. Two characters in the play, Vladimir and Estragon, do nothing other than wait endlessly but in vain for *Godot* to arrive.

under the title 'the way forward'. Reflecting back on our past research, we realize that we were often naïve and too ambitious to give prescriptive recommendations, spelling out what we thought should be done but without complementary analysis or reflection on the dynamics of policy change and the effort required to implement the recommendation that we gave. For example, Khayesi (1990: 221) gave the following recommendations:

> ... the conventional public service vehicle does not adequately meet the rural transport needs. The public service vehicles operate mainly on the classified road system and not the local route system. It is therefore necessary to develop appropriate transport modes for rural areas not only in Kakamega District but also other parts of Kenya. These modes should be made available at affordable prices. Faculties of engineering at the national universities and the technology institutes should take up this challenge.

As it can be noted, the actions recommended here do not make any reference to what it will take to implement them. This approach to providing recommendations partly reflects our understanding of the research-policy interface as consisting of separate phases where a researcher independently conducts a study and passes on the findings to policy makers at the end of the study. In several cases, researchers continue to organize worshops at the end of projects to disseminate findings to policy makers and other interested parties. Further, researchers publish their findings in journals and books, expecting policy makers to draw on these findings or recommendations to develop solutions. While we applaud these genuine efforts on the part of researchers, our experience over the years has taught us that there is much more to the use of findings than end-of-project disemination workshops or scientific publications. Researchers are faced with high demands from universities, requiring them to publish constantly in what has come to be known as "publish or perish" scholarship. It would be unfair or unrealistic to expect most researchers to devote a lot of time to policy dialogues and public involvement when their tenure assessment focuses largely on what they publish in top scientific journals.

Are we saying that researchers should not give recommendations or propose lines of actions? Absolutely not. We are simply arguing that recommendations need to be placed within the context of implementation or alternatively, the process of translating evidence into solutions needs to encourage policy makers, practitioners and researchers to interact and jointly define how research findings will be utilized in programme development.

Our research-policy interface learning curve has taught us that the process of translating knowledge into policy solutions is more complex than merely providing recommendations. It involves interactions and negotiations among several institutions and people responsible for knowledge generation, making policy decisions, developing solutions, implementing and evaluating the solutions (Bremer 2013). As pointed out by Marin and Delgado (2013), there are several hypotheses that are possible in science-policy interface. However, the choice of which hypothesis to support is dependent on the political, social and economic forces at work. We learn from their study of policy response in an ecological change situation that analysis of scientific evidence in a policy process is not a neutral undertaking.

Zohlnhöfer (2009) has also pointed out that although all different kinds of actors and events may trigger policy change, formally they need to be adopted by governments and parliaments, showing that policy change is a political issue as much as it may have technological, social and environmental aspects. With this insight, we are therefore avoiding the route of being too naïve in quickly recommending such options such as training matatu operators on customer care and the public on their rights or simply recommending that the matatu industry needs to be integrated into a bus rapid transit system. These measures and possibilities are necessary as we have shown in the preceding chapters but they need to be sustained over time and not be implemented in a reactive manner, and likely dropped after a short period of time.

We recognize that change can begin in a small way but we are also aware that if this change is not sustained, the effect tends to be short-lived. We are therefore inviting the different stakeholders involved in the matatu industry to continually engage in a dialogue to share their perspectives, including the knowledge contained in this book, and work out solutions not only for this industry but also for a viable transport system in Kenya. The matatu industry is only a part of the broader transport system. As has been demonstrated by Kahane (2012), for such a dialogue to occur, there is a need for all parties involved not only to create a safe space for dialogue, but, also to elevate the settings for the dialogue by creating courageous space that can allow the individuals involved to openly talk, listen and seek solutions to improve the transport system in Kenya.

Some key questions that may need to be addressed if an engaging dialogue is to be generated and sustained are: What transport system does Kenya aspire to have with respect to social, economic and ecological principles of sustainability? What pathways will be pursued to realize this system? What is the commitment to a sustainable transport system in current Kenyan planning and political strategies such as Vision 2030, Integrated National Transport Strategy and Devolution of Governance? Research points out that some countries are leading in the process of Africa rising or emerging (Radelet 2010): is Kenya taking significant steps to rise with regard to transport, matatu entrepreneurship, politics and its economy, or will future generations ask us what we did at a critical moment like this one?

We wish to conclude by looking at the issue of harnessing resources within and/or out of a nation state for local development. One of the issues raised in this regard is how to develop and tap into existing human, social, financial and natural capital and use it constructively and sustainably to improve the quality of life. While many African and developing countries often talk about the lack of capital as a key constraint, some studies or scholars are challenging this perspective by arguing and even demonstrating that these countries have the necessary capital, which may be hidden or dead[2] as de Soto (2000) and Moyo (2009) have put it. Matatu entrepreneurship has demonstrated and provided a platform for dead capital to be channelled into investment. The same process of releasing dead capital has been attributed to the informal sector in Kenya and other developing countries, and there has been a call for the creation of a conducive institutional and policy environment to enable more capital release (Kinyanjui 2012, Hart 2008, McCormick et al. 2007, McCormick 1999). There are also principles that have been identified from these innovative efforts in countries like India and which can be utilized by different sectors (Radjou, Prabhu and Ahuja 2012). The principles include seeking opportunity in adversity, doing more with less, thinking and acting flexibly, keeping it simple, including the margin and following the heart (Radjou, Prabhu and Ahuja 2012).

As the public and policy makers reflect on the matatu entrepreneurship, overall national development and the transport system desired, an observation by de Soto (2000: 37) may be helpful to them: 'Leaders of the Third World and former communist nations need not wander the world's foreign ministries and international financial institutions seeking their fortune. In the midst of their own poorest neighbourhoods and shanty towns, there are – if not acres of diamonds – trillions of dollars, all ready to be put to use if only the mystery of how assets are transformed into live capital can be unravelled'.

The initiative undertaken by the matatu industry to organize itself to be part and parcel of advocating for peaceful general elections in Kenya shows that with determination, the energy of this sector and Kenyans can be mobilized to achieve positive results (see Box 10.1). As the quotation above from de Soto shows, Kenya does not necessarily need to wander around the world looking for solutions. It has accumulated a fair amount of knowledge and practices that it can systematically implement to create a sustainable transport system and a high quality of life for its citizens. Kenya's Vision 2030 policy strategy aspires to see a Kenya firmly interconnected through a network of roads, railways, ports, airports, water and sanitation facilities, and telecommunications by 2030 (Government of the Republic of Kenya 2007: 6). We believe this aspiration for transport provides a basis for the kind of strategic dialogue we have argued for in the preceding paragraphs.

---

2   Dead capital refers to low or lost value of assets because they are held in forms that cannot be used easilyto generate wealth, for example, houses built on land whose ownership rights are not adequately recorded (de Soto 2000: 5–6)

Box 10.1

Matatus for Peaceful Elections Project

The violence that followed the announcement of presidential results in the 2007 general elections in Kenya made many people and institutions take initiatives to avoid a similar occurrence in future general elections. In 2013, Kenya held another general election. There were several efforts and initiatives meant to ensure these elections were peaceful. There was even a huge rally at Uhuru Park in Nairobi, attended by all of the presidential candidates, who promised to accept the results or take the appropriate legal course of action should they be dissatisfied with the election process.

The matatu industry joined the efforts at peaceful elections by mobilizing its operators under an initiative known as the Matatu for Peaceful Elections Project to spread this message to the public. The initiative was a joint project of the Matatu Welfare Association and the Matatu Drivers' and Conductors' Welfare Association. The main objective of this project, according to the Matatu Drivers and Conductors Welfare Association website, was 'to promote integrity in leadership and advocate for peace and stability in the run up to the 2013 general Elections by disseminating peace messages through the mass (matatu) public transport system' (Matatu Drivers and Conductors Welfare Association 2014). The target audience of the message was not only the matatu operators but also the public. The logic of practice behind this project was to use the matatu industry, a major component of Kenya's socio-economic fabric and one that most Kenyans identify with, to advocate peace and unity among Kenyans to maintain a peaceful environment before, during and after the general election period. This would ensure that a repeat of the 2007 post-election violence was avoided. As shown in Chapter 3, in the past workers in the matatu industry have been used to help incite violence, transporting large numbers of people who are out to cause violence, transporting offensive weapons and spreading provocative verbal and written messages. In the case of the peaceful election initiative, the logic was to use the same sector but for a peaceful objective.

The project, which ran from 1 October 2012 to 31 December 2012 was undertaken in collaboration with cooperation with various state agencies, including the Kenya Police Service, Transport Licensing Board, National Security Intelligence Service, and National Cohesion and Integration Commission. The initiative used three main strategies to pursue its objective:

- Placing stickers on matatu vehicles with messages calling for peaceful elections. All matatu workers and investors were required to preach peace, affix peace stickers on their vehicles, and engage their customers and members of the public in discussions on the benefits of maintaining peace and unity in Kenya. They were also required to reject requests to transport offensive weapons as well as people likely to cause violence or disseminate offensive or provocative written and verbal messages.

- Requiring matatu operators to adhere to a code of conduct (see details below); and
- Providing telephone hotline numbers through which members of the public would report any breach of the Matatus' Code of Conduct by any Public Service Vehicle during this period. All matatu workers and investors were encouraged to report any events likely to disturb the peace or anyone behaving in a manner likely to disturb the peace to the Matatu for Peaceful Elections Project Secretariat on a dedicated mobile number by sending a text message or calling. The Secretariat would then pass on the information to the relevant state agency and follow up to ensure action had been taken.

The Matatu for Peaceful Election Project developed a code of conduct for vehicle owners (investors), matatu SACCOs and companies, drivers and conductors. The details are indicated below.

Owners

- Shall allow MPE Project stickers to be affixed to their vehicles at no cost to the project.
- Shall not allow their vehicles to carry offensive weapons or transport people suspected to be planning violence or any disturbance to peace.
- Shall not allow their vehicles to be fitted with politically offensive messages, tribal messages or messages offensive to the society or individuals.
- Shall report the occurrence, observation or credible suspicion of unlawful activities to the MPE Project Secretariat or directly to state security agencies such as Police, Criminal Investigations Department (CID), National Cohesion and Integration Commission (NCIC) or the Chief's Office.
- Shall encourage their drivers, conductors and SACCO or Company staff to participate in the MPE Project activities.
- Shall discipline any driver or conductor, under their management, who violates this code of conduct in line with the rules and regulations of employment or report serious violations to the relevant state security agency and the MPE Project Secretariat.
- Shall employ disciplined, properly trained, tested and qualified drivers.
- Shall employ disciplined and licensed conductors.

- Shall keep records of their employees who will be registered with the SACCO office.
- Shall not engage in corrupt practices. They shall report all cases of law enforcement corruption and harassment to the MPE Project Secretariat.

SACCOs and Companies

- Shall promote harmony and discipline on their routes at all times.
- Shall be vigilant and not allow vehicles under their management to be used for unlawful activities.
- Shall encourage drivers and conductors under their management to participate in MPE Project Activities.
- Shall allow MPE Project peace stickers to be affixed on vehicles under their management at no cost to the project.
- Shall report any suspected unlawful activities or individuals suspected of committing or planning to commit unlawful activities. Reports shall be made to the MPE Project Secretariat or directly to state security agencies such as Police, Criminal Investigations Department (CID), National Cohesion and Integration Commission (NCIC) or the Chief's Office.
- Shall discipline any investor, driver, conductor, SACCO or Company employee under the SACCO's or Company's management who violates this code of conduct in line with the rules and regulations of the SACCO or Company or report serious violations to the relevant state security agency and the MPE Project Secretariat.

Drivers

- Shall discourage heated debates in their vehicles, likely to cause verbal or physical violence.
- Shall not play politically offensive music or recorded messages or such music or recorded messages likely to incite tribal or factional animosity.
- Shall affix and maintain MPE Project stickers on their vehicles without cost to the project.
- Shall show respect to all commuters regardless of their age, gender, social status, religion, tribe or any other natural properties, and transport them in their vehicles at all times when they request, on agreed terms.
- Shall not permit drivers and conductors not authorized by the owners, SACCO or company managers to operate vehicles under their control.
- Shall be vigilant to observe and report cases of suspected unlawful activities or individuals suspected of committing or planning to

commit unlawful activities. The drivers shall report to the MPE
Project Secretariat or directly to state security agencies such
as Police, Criminal Investigations Department (CID), National
Cohesion and Integration Commission (NCIC) or the Chief's Office.

- Shall promote unity, respect and cohesion
  among all their customers at all times.
- Shall always be in uniform, be sober, clean and presentable.
- Shall not smoke, chew khat (miraa), drink alcoholic
  substances or take any drugs while on duty (if he/she
  must take drugs for medical reasons which may cause
  drowsiness or misjudgment then he/she must not drive).
- Shall observe the Highway Code and traffic
  rules and regulations at all times.
- Shall take passengers to their final destination.
- Shall not permit unauthorized (squad) drivers to handle their vehicles.
- Shall not engage in corrupt practices. They shall
  report all cases of law enforcement corruption and
  harassment to the MPE Project Secretariat.

Conductors

- Shall avoid inciting other colleagues in issues that
  may result to disturbance of the peace.
- Shall exercise self control to avoid escalating conflict by
  remaining calm and calling on their customers to remain
  calm during situations of developing conflict.
- Shall charge, collect the prevailing fare and drop passengers
  at designated bus stops and final destinations.
- Shall be vigilant to observe and report cases of suspected unlawful
  activities or individuals suspected of committing or planning to
  commit unlawful activities. The conductors shall report to the
  MPE Project Secretariat or directly to state security agencies such
  as Police, Criminal Investigations Department (CID), National
  Cohesion and Integration Commission (NCIC) or the Chief's Office.
- Shall be in full official uniform at all times when on duty.
- Shall be in possession of PSV conductors' licence, current
  certificate of good conduct and badge from KRA.
- Shall observe the Highway Code and traffic regulations at all times.
- Shall not engage in corrupt practices. They shall
  report all cases of law enforcement corruption and
  harassment to the MPE Project Secretariat.

Source: Matatu Welfare Association, and Matatu Drivers and Conductors Welfare
Association (2014).

Summary

The key points of this chapter are as follows:

- How do we create a work environment for the matatu industry to thrive and how do we develop professionalism among people working in the matatu industry?
- How do we create a transaction space that allows matatu passengers to question how they are treated and demand a quality service for which they are paying?
- How do we develop and sustain national dialogues on the relevance of the matatu industry to Kenyan society as well as pursuing practically the aspirations for development as articulated in strategies such as Vision 2030?

References

Abler, R., Adams, J.S. and Gould, P. 1972. *Spatial Organization: The Geographer's View of the World.* London: Prentice-Hall International, Inc.

Aduwo, I.G. 1990. The role, efficiency and quality of service of the matatu mode of public transport in Nairobi: a geographical analysis. MA. University of Nairobi.

Alila, P.O. 2001. Micro- and small-enterprises: Policies and development. In *Negotiating Social Space: East African Micro Enterprises*, 329–344. Edited by P.O. Alila and P.O. Pedersen. Trenton, New Jersey: Africa World Press.

Alila, P., Khayesi, M., Odhiambo, W. and Pedersen, P.O. 2007. Trade and transport: Business linkages and networks. In *Business in Kenya: Institutions and Interactions*, 281–309. Edited by D. McCormick, P.O. Alila and M. Omosa. Nairobi: University of Nairobi Press.

Anderson, D.M. 2002. Vigilantes, violence and the politics of public order in Kenya. *African Affairs*, 101 (405): 531–555.

Asingo, P.O. and Mitullah, W. 2005. *Implementing road transport safety measures in Kenya: policy issues and challenges.* Nairobi: Institute for Development Studies, University of Nairobi.

Ardila-Gómez, A. 2004. Transit planning in Curitiba and Bogotá: roles in interaction, risk, and change. Ph. D. Massachusetts Institute of Technology.

Ashby, W.R. 2004. Principles of the self-organizing system. *E:CO*, 6 (1–2): 102–126.

Attoh, S.A. 2010. Urban geography of Sub-Saharan Africa. In *Geography of Sub-Saharan Africa*, 265–304. Edited by S.A. Attoh. New York: Prentice Hall.

Banister, D. 2005. *Unsustainable Transport: City Transport in the new Century.* London: Routledge.

Behrens, R. 2011. Paratransit futures in African cities. In *10 Years with the FUT Programme*, 92–101. Edited by Volvo Research and Educational Foundation. Göteborg: Volvo Research and Educational Foundation.

Behrens, R., McCormick, D. and Mfinanga, D. editors. 2014. *Paratransit in African Cities. London*: Earthscan Publications Ltd (forthcoming).

Bontis, N. 2002. *World Congress on Intellectual Capital Readings.* Boston: Butterworth Heinemann.

Bourdieu, P.1990. *The Logic of Practice* (Translated into English by Richard Nice). California: Sanford University Press.

Branson, R. 2009. *Screw it, let's do it: Lessons in Life and Business.* London: Virgin Books.

Bremer, S. 2013. Mobilising high-quality knowledge through dialogic environmental governance: a comparison of approaches and their institutional settings. *International Journal of Sustainable Development*, 16 (1–2): 66–90.

Brubaker, R. 1993. Social theory as habitus. In *Critical Perspectives*, 212–234. Edited by C. Calhoun, E. LiPuma and M. Postone. Chicago: University of Chicago Press.

Bwisa, H.M. and Nafukho, F.M. 2012. *Learning Entrepreneurship through Indigenous Knowledge*. Oakville, Ontario: Nsemia Publishers.

Carland, J.W., Carland, J.C. and Ensley, M.D. 2001. Hunting the heffalump: the theoretical basis and dimensionality of the Carland entrepreneurship index. *Academy of Entrepreneurship Journal*, 7 (2): 51–84.

Carson, R. 1962. *Silent Spring*. New York: Penguin Books.

Central Bureau of Statistics, International Centre for Economic Growth and K-Rep Holdings Ltd. 1999. *National micro and small enterprise baseline survey 1999: survey results*. Nairobi: Central Bureau of Statistics.

Cervero, R. 1998. *The Transit Metropolis: A Global Inquiry*. Washington, DC: Island Press.

Cervero, R. and Golub, A. 2007. Informal transport: a global perspective. *Transport Policy*, 14 (6): 445–457.

Cervero, R. 2000. *Informal Transport in the Developing World. Nairobi:* United Nations Centre for Human Settlements.

Chambers, R. 1983. *Rural Development: Putting the Last First*. London: Pearson Education Limited.

Chambers, R. 2005. *Whose Reality counts: Putting the Last First*. Bourton-on-Dunsmore: Intermediate Technology Development Group Publishing.

Chitere, P. and Kibua, T. 2004. Efforts to improve road safety in Kenya: achievements and limitations of reforms in the matatu industry. Sub-Saharan Africa Transport Policy (SSATP) Annual Meeting. Addis Ababa, Ethiopia, 25 Sptember-1 October 2004.

Clark, B. 1998. *Political Economy: A Comparative Approach*. Westport: Praeger Publishers.

Collins, J. 2001. *Good to Great: Why some Companies make the Leap ... and others don't*. New York: Harper Press.

Crang, M., Hughes, A. and Gregson, N. et al. 2013. Rethinking governance and value in commodity chains through global recycling networks. *Transactions of the Institute of British Geographers*, 38: 12–24 doi: 10.1111/j.1475-5661.2012.00515.x

Crossan, M.M., Lane, H.W. and White, R.E. 1999. An organisational learning framework: From intuition to institution. *Academy of Management Review*, 24 (3): 522–37.

Darkoh, M.B.K. 2014. Social and environmental science research in support of a policy definition of the "Future we Want" in Africa. *Development*, 56 (3): 387–395.

De Soto, H. 1989. *The other Path: The Invisible Revolution in the Third World.* New York: Harper and Row Publishers.

De Soto, H. 2000. *The Mystery of Capital: Why Capitalism triumphs in the West and fails everywhere else.* New York: Basic Books.

Department for International Development. 2009. *Political economy analysis: how to note.* London: Department for International Development.

Dyer, L. and Ericksen, J. 2005. *Achieving marketplace agility through human resource scalability.* Ithaca: Cornell University: Center for dvanced Human Resource Studies, School of Industrial and Labour Relations.

Edward, K. and Aregay, W. 2014. Ethnic diversity and federalism: a comparative analysis of Ethiopia and Kenya. The 13th International Conference of Africanists, Moscow, 27–30 May 2014.

Edward, K and Hayoz, N. 2014. Ethnicity and constitution making in Kenya's long walk to democratic transition. The 13th International Conference of Africanists, Moscow, 27–30 May 2014.

Dilts, R. 2014. *NLP and Self Organization Theory.* [Online]. Available at: http://www.nlpu.com/Articles/artic23.htm [Accessed on 19 January 2014].

Easterly, W. 2006. *The Whiteman's Burden: Why the West's Efforts to Aid the rest have done so much ill and so little good.* Oxford: Oxford University Press.

Etherington, K. and Simon, D. 1996. Paratransit and employment in Phnom Penh: the dynamics and development potential of *cyclo* riding. *Journal of Transport Geography*, 4 (1): 37–53.

Eyben, R. 2013. *Uncovering the Politics of 'Evidence' and 'Results': A Framing Paper for Development Practitioners.* [Online].Available at: http://bigpushforward.net/wp-content/uploads/2011/01/Uncovering-the-Politics-of-Evidence-and-Results-by-Rosalind-Eyben.pdf [Accessed on 19 April 2014].

Gardner, H. 2006. *Five Minds for the Future.* Boston: Harvard Business School Press.

Giddens, A. 1984. *The Constitution of Society.* Cambridge: Polity Press.

Godard, X. 2007. The contribution of informal transport to urban mobility. *Villes en Développement*, 78: 3–5.

Goety, A.R., Vowles, T.M. and Tierney, S. 2009. Bridging the qualitative-quantitative divide in Transport Geography. *The Professional Geographer*, 61 (3): 323–335.

Government of Kenya. 2003. *Kenya: economic recovery strategy for wealth and employment creation 2003–2007.* Nairobi: Government of Kenya.

Government of the Republic of Kenya. 2007. *Kenya: Vision 2030.* Nairobi: Ministry of Planning and National development.

Graeff, J. 2009. The organization, issues and the future role of matatu industry in Nairobi, Kenya. New York: Centre for Sustainable Urban Development, Earth Institute, University of Columbia.

Graham, F. 2010. M-Pesa: Kenya's mobile wallet revolution. [Online]. Available at: http://scholar.google.com/scholar?q=Graham+2010+M-Pesa&btnG=&hl=en&as_sdt=0%2C44&as_vis=1 [Accessed on 6 April 2014].

Graham, C.M. and Nafukho, F.M. 2007. Culture, organizational learning and selected independent variables in small-size business enterprises. *Journal of European Industrial Training*, 31 (2): 127–144.

Greene, R. 2012. *Mastery*. London: Profile Books Limited.

Grieco, M. 2008. *Transportation and Society – with special reference to Africa*. [Online]. Available at: http://transportandsociety.com/seminar.html [Accessed on 21 April 2014].

Hart, K. 2008. *Between bureaucracy and the people: a political history of informality*. Copenhagen: Danish Institute for International Studies (Working Paper 2008/27).

Han, S.S. 2010. Managing motorization in sustainable transport planning: the Singapore experience. *Journal of Transport Geography*, 18 (2): 314–321.

Helbing, D., Molnár, P., Farkas, I.J. et al. 2001. Self-organizing pedestrian movement. *Environment and Planning B: Planning and Design*, 28 (3): 361–383.

Hill, M. 1975. *The roots of Harambee*. Nairobi: Kenyatta University College, *Bureau* of Educational Research (Occasional Paper No. 3011).

Hilling, D. 1996. *Transport and Developing Countries*. London: Routledge.

Howe, J. 2001. The headloading and footpath economy – walking in Sub-Saharan Africa. *World Transport Policy and Practice*, 7 (4): 8–12.

Howe, J. and Bryceson, D. 2000. *Poverty and Urban Transport in East Africa: Review of Research and Dutch Donor Experience*. The Hague: International Institute for Infrastructural, Hydraulic and Environmental Engineering.

Hoyle, B.S. and Knowles, R.D. (eds) 2001. *Modern Transport Geography*. Chichester: John Wiley & Sons.

Hughes, N. and Lonie, S. 2007. M-PESA: mobile money for the "unbanked" turning cell phones into 24-hour tellers in Kenya. *Innovations*, 2 (1–2): 63–81.

Ignacio, M. and Radcliffe, D. 2010. Mobile payments go viral: M-Pesa in Kenya. [Online]. Available at: http://siteresources.worldbank.org/AFRICAEXT/Resources/258643–1271798012256/M-PESA_Kenya.pdf [Accessed on 21 April 2014]

Institute for Transportation and Development Policy. 2005. Bus rapid transit in Dar es Salaam. [Online]. Available at: http://www.itdp.org/programs/dar/home.aspx [Accessed on 16 April 2005].

Irungu, K.Z. 2007. *Nairobi urban transportation challenges – learning from Japan*. JICA Training Course: Comprehensive Urban Transportation Planning and Project.

Jack, W. and Suri, T. (2010). The economics of M-Pesa. [Online]. Available at: http://www.mit.edu/~tavneet/M-PESA.pdf [Accessed on 6 April 2014].

Jenkins, R. 1992. *Pierre Bourdieu*. London: Routledge.

Jirón, P. 2011. Mobility practices in Santiago de Chile: the consequences of restricted urban accessibility. In *The Politics of Proximity: Mobility and Immobility in Practice*, 133–151. Edited by G. Pellegrino. Surrey: Ashgate.

Johnson, S. 1999. *Who moved my Cheese? An amazing way to deal with Change in your Work and in your Life*. London: Vermillon.

Journeys. 2011. *Passenger transport mode shares in world cities*. [Online]. Available at:http://ltaacademy.gov.sg/doc/J11Nov-p60PassengerTransportModeSHares.pdf [Accessed on 12 April 2014].

Juma, C. 2011. *The New Harvest: Agricultural Innovation in Africa*. Oxford: Oxford University Press.

Kahane, A. 2012. *Transformative Scenario Planning: Working together to change the Future*. San Francisco: Berrett-Koehler Publishers, Inc.

Kamuhanda, R. and Schmidt, O. 2009. Matatu: a case study of the core segment of the public transport market of Kampala, Uganda. *Transport Reviews*, 29 (1): 129–142.

Kanyama, A and Cars, G. 2009. *In search of a framework for institutional coordination in the planning for public transportation in sub-Saharan African cities: An analysis based on experiences from Dar-es-Salaam and Nairobi*. Stockholm: Royal Institute of Technology.

Kahl, C.H. 1998. Population growth, environmental degradation, and state-sponsored violence: the case of Kenya, 1991–93. *International Security*, 23 (2): 80–119.

Kaira, C.K. 1983. *Transportation needs of the rural population in developing countries: an approach to improved transportation planning*. Ph.D. Karlsruhe University.

Kariuki, J. 2013. Survey finds savers prefer banking on mobile phones. *Daily Nation*, [Online]. Available at: http://www.businessdailyafrica.com/Survey-finds-savers-prefer-banking-on-mobile-phones/-/539552/1707866/-/3nw8mjz/-/index.html. [Accessed on 22 April 2013].

Kapila, S., Manu, M. and Lamba, D. 1982. *The matatu mode of public transportation in metropolitan Nairobi*. Nairobi: Mazingira Institute.

Kayi, C. 2007. *An analysis of road traffic accidents using geographic information systems (GIS): The case of Nairobi city, Kenya*. Hamburg: Verlag Dr. Kovac.

Kebero, A.J. 1979. The working conditions of drivers and conductors employed in urban transport services. *The Transporter*, 2: 42–51.

Kebir, L. and Crevoisier, O. 2008. Cultural resources and regional development: the case of the cultural legacy of watchmaking. *European Planning Studies*, 16 (9): 1189–1205.

Kemuma, J. 2000. The past and the future in the present: Kenyan adult immigrant's stories on orientation and adult education in Sweden. Ph. D. Uppsala University.

Kemuma, J., Murunga, G.R. and Khayesi, M. 2002. Matatu youth in Kenya: a "notorious workforce?" Youth Policy and the Policies of Youth in Africa Conference. United States of America, Evanston, Northwestern University, 10–11 May 2002.

Kemuma, J. 2007. Life history methodology: a tool for (studying lives) (re)constructing a multiplicity of stories in different socio-cultural, economic and political spaces. In *Livshistorieforskning og kvalitative interview*, 308–332. Edited by P.K. Anna, G. Stinne and L. Vibeke. Danmark: PUC CVU Midt-vest.

Kemuma J. 2012. Gender intersects: African women negotiate visibility from spaces of invisibility in Sweden. In *Invisible Girl*. Edited by G.M. Frånberg, C. Hällgren, Camilla and E. Dunkels. Umeå: Umeå University.

Kenya Bus Service Management Ltd. 2014. Abiria card. [Online]. Available at: http://www.kenyabus.net/abiria/ [Accessed on 21 April 2014].

Kenya Mpya. 2014. Nairobi County: background information. [Online]. Available at: http://www.kenyampya.com/index.php?county=Nairobi&page=Backgrou nd_Information [Accessed on 21 April 2014].

Kenya National Bureau of Statistics. 2014. Kenya: key facts and figures. [Online]. Available at:

http://www.knbs.or.ke/index.php?option=com_phocadownload&view=category &id=20&Itemid=595 [Accessed on 21 April 2014].

Kilby, P. 1971. Hunting the heffalump. In *Entrepreneurship and Economic Development*, 1–40. Edited by P. Kilby. New York: The Free Press.

Kilby. P. 2003. The heffalump revisited. *Journal of International Entrepreneurship*, 1 (1): 13–29.

Kimani, D.P., Kibua, T.N. and Masinde, M. 2004. *The role of the matatu industry in Kenya: economic costs, benefits and policy concerns*. Nairobi: Institute of Policy Analysis and Research (Discussion Paper No. 053/2004).

Kipkorir, B. 1981. Historical perspectives of development. In *Kerio Valley: Past, Present and Future*, 1–11. Edited by B.E. Kipkorir, R. Soper and J.S. Ssenyonga. Nairobi: Eleza Services Limited.

Khayesi, M. 1990. The road network pattern and household travel characteristics in Kakamega district: a geographical analysis. MA. Kenyatta University.

Khayesi, M. 1993. Rural household travel characteristics: the case of Kakamega district. *Journal of Eastern African Research and Development*, 23: 88–105.

Khayesi, M. 1995. Analysis of the pattern of the road network in Kakamega district. *Journal of Eastern Africa Research and Development*, 25: 104–119.

Khayesi, M. 1997. *Matatu workers in Nairobi, Thika and Ruiru towns, Kenya: analysis of their socio-economic characteristics, career patterns and conditions of work*. Nairobi: University of Nairobi, Institute for Development Studies.

Khayesi, M. 1999. The struggle for regulatory and economic sphere of influence in the matatu means of transport in Kenya: a stakeholder analysis. The Sixth International Conference on Competition and Ownership in Land Passenger Transport, South Africa, Cape Town, 19–23 September 1999.

Khayesi, M. 2001a. Matatu workers in Nairobi, Thika and Ruiru: Career patterns and conditions of work. In *Negotiating Social Space: East African Micro Enterprises*, 69–96. Edited by P.O. Alila and P.O. Pedersen. Trenton, New Jersey: Africa World Press.

Khayesi, M. 2001b. *Impacts of interventions in bee-keeping and irrigation on household welfare in the Kerio Basin Development Zone, Kenya*. Addis Ababa: Organisation for Social Science Research in Eastern and Southern Africa.

Khayesi, M. and Ogonda, R.T. 2001. Trends and progress in transport studies in Kenya. Draft.

Khayesi, M. 2002. Struggle for socio-economic niche and control in the matatu industry in Kenya, *Development Policy and Management Forum Bulletin*, IX (2): 1–12.

Khayesi, M. 2004. Partnership and dialogue for implementation of new road safety rules in Kenya. *African Safety Promotion: A Journal of Injury Prevention and Violence Prevention*, 2 (2): 35–42.

Khayesi, M. 2010. *Road Safety in Kenya: Policy and Intervention Measures.* Saarbrücken: Verlag Dr. Muller Publishing House Ltd.

Khayesi, M., Monheim, H. and Nebe, J.M. 2010. Negotiating 'streets for all' in urban transport planning: the case for pedestrians, cyclists and street vendors in Nairobi, Kenya. *Antipode: A Radical Journal of Geography*, 42 (1): 103–126.

Khayesi, M., Amekudzi, A. and Klopp, J. 2012. Pursuing alternatives to urban automobile dependence path: a comparative analysis of Zurich and Singapore. Models of Mobility, Systemic Differences, Path Dependencies, Economic, Social and Environmental, Impact (1900 to tomorrow) Workshop, Canada, York University, 23–24 March 2012.

Khayesi, J. and Nafukho, F.M. 2011. Entrepreneurship and career development in Africa: State of the Art. *Career Planning and Adult Development Journal*, 27 (1): 126–137.

Khosa, M.M. 1991. Routes, ranks and rebels: feuding in the taxi revolution. *Journal of South African Studies*, 18 (1): 232–251.

Khosa, M.M. 1993. Transport and the 'Taxi Mafia' in South Africa. *The Urban Age*, 2 (1): 8–9.

Khosa, M.M. 1995. Transport and popular struggles in South Africa. *Antipode*, 27 (2): 167–188.

Khosa, M.M. 1997. Sisters on slippery wheels: Women taxi drivers in South Africa. *Transformations*, 33: 18–33.

Knoflacher, H. 2009. From myth to science in urban and transport planning: From uncontrolled to controlled and responsible urban development in transport planning. *International Journal of Injury Control and Safety Promotion*, 16 (1): 3–7.

Kinyanjui, M. 2010. *Social relations and associations in the informal sector in Kenya.* Geneva: United Nations Research Institute for Social Development (Social Policy Development Paper Number 43).

Kinyanjui, M.N. 2012. *Vyama, Institutions of hope: Ordinary People's Market Coordination and Society Organization.* Oakville, Ontario, Canada: Nsemia Inc. Publishers.

Kinyanjui, M. and Khayesi, M. 2005. *Social capital, micro and small enterprises and poverty-alleviation in East Africa.* Addis Ababa: Organisation for Social Science Research in Eastern and Southern Africa.

Kinyanjui, M. and Khayesi, M. 2013. Exploiting Opportunities in the Matatu Service for Transport Planning in Nairobi, Kenya. In *(Re)membering Kenya:*

Interrogating Marginalization and Governance, 170–187. Edited by G. Gona and M. wa Mungai. Nairobi: Twaweza Communications Ltd.

Kioy, D. 2011. *Matatu Entrepreneurs: A Study on Investors in Kenya's Informal Transport Business*. Saarbrücken: Lambert Academic Publishing.

Klopp, J.M. 2012. Towards a political economy of transport policy and practice in Nairobi. *Urban Forum*, 23: 1–12.

Klopp, J., Mutua, J., Orwa, D., Waiganjo, P., White, A. and Williams, S. n.d. Towards a Standard for Paratransit? Lessons from developing a GTFS Data for Nairobi's Matatu System. [Online]. Available at: https://docs.google.com/file/d/0B8U8tJgDCqhhVlBsTXRDVHZUS3M/edit?pli=1 [Accessed on 18 May 2014].

Koglin, T. and Rye, T. 2014. The marginalization of bicycling in Modernist urban transport planning. *Journal of Transport & Health*, 1: 214–222.

Krug, E., Dahlberg, L.L., Mercy, J.A., Zwi, A.B. and Lozano, R. eds. 2002. *World Report on Violence and Health*. Geneva: World Health Organization.

Kwakye, E.A., Fouracre, P.R. and Ofosu-Dorte, D. 1997. Developing strategies to meet the transport needs of the urban poor in Ghana. *World Transport Policy & Practice*, 3 (1): 8–14.

Lam, S.H. and Toan, T.D. 2006. Land transport policy and public transport in Singapore. *Transportation*, 33 (2): 171–188.

Lee-Smith, D. 1989. Urban management in Nairobi: case study of the matatu mode of public transport. In *African Cities in Crisis: Managing Rapid Urban Growth*, 274–304. Edited by R.E. Stren and R.R. White. Boulder: Westview Press.

Lowe, J.C. and Moryadas, S. 1975. *The Geography of Movement*. Hoston: Houghton Mifflin Company.

Lucas, K. and Currie, G. 2011. Developing socially inclusive transportation policy: transferring the United Kingdom policy approach to the State of Victoria? *Transportation* (DOI 10.1007/s11116–011–9324–2).

Maathai, W. 2006. *Unbowed: A Memoir*. New York: Alfred Knopf Publishing Group

Macharia, K. 1987. The role of social network and the state in the urban informal sector in Nairobi. In *Selected Economic Development Issues in Eastern and Southern Africa*, 262–305. Edited by K. Macharia, A. Naho, S.R. Shabalala and F.C. Shechambo. Nairobi: International Development Research Centre.

Mahajan, V. 2009. *Africa Rising: How 900 Million African Consumers offer more than you think*. New Jersey Prentice Hall.

Makura, M. 2011. *Africa's Greatest Entrepreneurs*. Johannesburg: Penguin Books.

Marin, V.H. and Delgado, L.E. 2013. From ecology to society and back: the (in)convenient hypothesis syndrome. *International Journal of Sustainable Development*, 16 (1–2): 46–64.

Marsick, V.J., and Watkins, K.E. 1996. A framework for the learning organisation. In *Action: Creating the learning organisation*, 3–12. Edited by J.J. Phillips, K.E. Watkins, and V.J. Marsick. Alexandria, Virginia: American Society for Training and Development Publications.

Matatu Welfare Association. 2014. Kitu Kodogo Out Project. [Online]. Available at: http://matatu.co.ke/kkop/projectdetails.php?v=kkop&projectid=1 [Accessed on 21 April 2014].

Matatu Welfare Association, and Matatu Drivers and Conductors Welfare Association. 2014. Matatus for Peaceful lections (MPE) Project. [Online]. Available at: http://www.matatu.co.ke/docs/MPE_Code-of-Conduct.pdf [Accessed on 21 April 2014].

May, A.D. 2004. Singapore: the development of a world class transport system. *Transport Reviews*, 24 (1): 79–101.

McCormick, D. 1999. African enterprise clusters and industrialization: Theory and reality. *World Development*, 27 (9): 1531–1551.

McCormick, D., Mitullah, W., Chitere, P., Orero, R. and Ommeh, M. 2013. Paratransit business strategies: a bird's-eye view of *matatus* in Nairobi. *Journal of Public Transportation*, 16 (2): 135–152.

McCormick, D., Kimuyu, P. and Kinyanjui, M.N. 2007. Textiles and clothing: Global players and local struggles. In *Business in Kenya: Institutions and Interactions*, 197–232. Edited by D. McCormick, P.O. Alila and M. Omosa. Nairobi: University of Nairobi Press.

McFarlane, C. 2008. Urban shadows: materiality, the 'Southern City' and urban theory. *Geography Compass*, 2 (2): 340–358.

Meredith, M. 2005. *The Fate of Africa: A History of Fifty Years of Independence*. New York: Public Affairs.

Midgley, P. 1994. *Urban transport in Asia: an operational agenda for the 1990s.* Washington, D.C.: World Bank (Technical Paper No. 224).

Moyo, D. 2009. Dead Aid: *Why Aid is Not Working and How There is Another Way for Africa*. London: Penguin Books.

Muiruri, M. 2012. Kenya: Uhuru contests phasing out 14-seater matatus. *Daily Nation on the Web*, [Online]. Available at: http://allafrica.com/stories/201201230012.html. [Accessed on 21 April 2014].

Mutisya, D. 1995. *The forgotten workers: The case of house helpers in Nairobi city, Kenya.* Addis Ababa: Organisation for Social Science Research for Eastern and Southern Africa.

Mutongi, K. 2006. Thugs or entrepreneurs? perceptions of matatu operators in Nairobi, 1970 to the present. *Africa*, 76 (4): 549–568.

Mutongi, K. 2014. Making *it in Nairobi: Matatu Culture and Political Economy in New Africa* Chicago: University of Chicago Press (forthcoming).

Murunga, G.R. 1999. Urban violence in Kenya's transition to pluralist politics, 1982–1992, Africa *Development*, XXIV(1 & 2): 165–198.

Murunga, G.R. 2005. Inherently unhygienic races: Plague and the origins of settler dominance in Nairobi, 1899–1907. In *African Urban Spaces in Historical Perspectives*, 98–130. Edited by S.J. Salm and T. Falola. Rochester, New York: University of Rochester Press.

Mwaniki, C. 2013. *M-Pesa grows to biggest Bank by Customer Deposits.* [Online]. Available at: http://www.businessdailyafrica.com/MPesa-grows-to-biggest-bank-by-customer-deposits/-/539552/1752126/-/15r12ao/-/index.html [Accessed on 22 April 2013].

Mwiria, K. 1986. *Education through self-help: The experience of the Kenya Harambee Secondary Schools.* Nairobi: Kenyatta University, Bureau of Educational Research.

Nafukho, M. 1994. Education through self-help: The case of Kenyan university students with the introduction of university fees payment. *Journal of Eastern African Research and Development,* 24: 42–53.

Nafukho, F.M. 2001. *The forgotten workers: The case of public Service vehicle drivers in Eldoret, Kenya.* Addis Ababa: Organization of Social Science Research in Eastern and Southern Africa.

Nafukho, F.M. and Khayesi, M. 2002. Livelihood, conditions of work, regulation and road safety in the small-scale public transport sector. In *Urban Mobility for All,* 241–245. Edited by X. Godard and Fatonzoun. Lisse, the Netherlands: A.A. Balkema Publishers.

Nafukho, F.M. and Hinton, E.B. 2003. Determining the relationship between driver's level of education, training and job performance in Kenya. *Human Resource Development Quarterly,* 14 (3): 265–283.

Nafukho, F.M., Amutabi, N.M., and Otunga, R.N. 2005. *Foundations of Adult Education in Africa.* Cape Town: UNESCO/Pearson Education.

Nafukho, F.M., Hinton, B.E. and Graham, C.M. 2007. A study of truck drivers and their job performance regarding highway safety. *Performance Improvement Quarterly,* 20 (1): 61–74.

Nafukho, F.M. 2008. Consensus building, dialogue and spirituality principles of the learning organisation paradigm: Implications for Kenya's public service reform agenda. *Journal of Third World Studies,* XXV (2): 153–175.

Nafukho, F.M., Graham, C.M., and Muyia, M.H. 2009. Determining the relationship among organisational learning dimensions of a small-size business enterprise. *Journal of European Industrial Training,* 33 (1): 32–51.

Nafukho, F.M. and Muyia, M.A.H. 2010. Entrepreneurship and socio-economic development in Africa: A reality or myth? *Journal of European Industrial Training,* 34 (2): 96–109.

Nafukho, F.M., Wawire, N.H.W. and Mungania, P. 2011. *Management of Adult Education Organizations in Africa.* Cape Town: Pearson Education and UNESCO.

Nantulya, V.M. and Muli-Musiime, F. 2001. Kenya: Uncovering the social determinants of road traffic accidents. In *Challenging Inequities: From Ethics to Action,* 211–225. *Edited by* T. Evans, M. Whitehead, F. Diderichsen, A. Bhuiya and M. Wirth. New York: Oxford University Press.

National Transport and Safety Authority Act 2013. Nairobi: Government Printer.

Ng'weno, H. 1984. Letter from the editor. *The Weekly Review,* 14 September, p. 1.

Ngowi, H.P. 2005. Private sector delivery of urban services: benefits, obstacles and ways forward for public transport service in Dar es Salaam city, Tanzania. *Eastern Africa Social Science Research Review,* XXI(1): 97–118.

Norwegian Nobel Committee. 2004. The Nobel Peace Prize for 2004. [Online]. Available at: http://nobelpeaceprize.org/en_GB/laureates/laureates-2004/ press-2004/ [Accessed on 8 November 2013].

Nutley, S., Powell, A. and Davies, H. 2012. *What counts as good evidence?* Provocation Paper for the Alliance for Useful Evidence (University of St Andrews, School of Management).

Nyong'o, A. 1981. The sociological transformation of Harambee: or is accumulation the source of political demobilization? In *Popular Participation and Rural Development*, 108–118. Edited by N. Ng'ethe. Nairobi: University of Nairobi, Institute for Development Studies (Occasional Paper No. 38).

Obama, B. 2004. *Dreams from my Father*. New York: Three Rivers Press.

Obama, B. 2006. *The Audacity of Hope*. New York: Three Rivers Press.

Obuya, P. and Agoya, V. 2013. Riots in city estate as woman shoved off matatu is run over. Daily Nation, [Online]. Available at: http://www.nation.co.ke/News/ Woman-dies-in-matatu-row-over-Sh10/-/1056/1671802/-/9leur9z/-/index. html [Accessed on 21 April 2014].

Odero, W., Khayesi, M. and Heda, P. 2003. Road traffic injuries in Kenya: Magnitude, causes and status of intervention. *Injury Control and Safety Promotion*, 10 (1): 53–61.

Odhiambo, W. and Mitullah, W. 2007. Policies and regulations for business development. In *Business in Kenya: Institutions and Interactions*, 40–63. Edited by D. McCormick, P.O. Alila and M. Omosa. Nairobi: University of Nairobi Press.

Ogonda, R.T. 1976. Transportation in Nairobi area: a geographical analysis. MA. University of Nairobi.

Ogonda, R. Timothy. 1986. The development of road system in Kenya. Ph. D. University of Nairobi.

Ortenblad, A. 2001. On differences between organizational learning and learning Organization. *The Learning Organization*, 8 (3): 125–133.

Ostrom, E. 2009. Polcycentric systems as one approach to solving collective-action problems. In *Climate change and sustainable development: new challenges for poverty reduction*, 17–35. Edited by M.A. Mohamed Salih. Cheltenham: Edward Elgar.

Ostrom, E. 2010. Beyond Markets and States: Polycentric Governance of Complex Economic Systems. *American Economic Review*, 100 (3): 1–33.

Perry, D.A. 1995. Self-organizing systems across scales. *TREE*, 10 (6): 241–244.

Piketty, T. 2014. Capital in the twenty-first century. Cambridge, Massachusetts: The Belknap Press of Harvard University Press.

Pinchot, G. and Pellman, R. 1999. *Intrapreneuring in Action: A Handbook for Business Innovation*. San Francisco: Berrett-Koehler Publishers, Inc.

Psacharopoulos, G. 1985. Returns to education: A further international update and implications. *Journal of Human Resources*, 20 (4): 583–604.

Psacharopoulos, G. 1994. Returns to investment in education: A global update. *World Development*, 22 (9):1325–43.

Radelet, S. 2010. *Emerging Africa: How 17 Countries are leading the Way.* Washington DC.: Center for Global Development.

Radjou, N., Prabhu, J. and Ahuja, S. 2012. *Jugaad innovation: think frugal, be flexible, generate breakthrough growth.* San Francisco: Jossey-Bass.

Rasmussen, J. 2012. Inside the system, outside the law: operating the matatu sector in Nairobi. *Urban Forum:* DOI 10.1007/s12132–012–9171-z.

Republic of Kenya. 2003. *Kenya Government Economic Recovery Strategy for Wealth and Employment Creation 2003–2007.* Nairobi: Government Printer.

Republic of Kenya. 2011. *Economic Survey.* Nairobi: Government Printer

Republic of Kenya. 2012. *Economic Survey.* Nairobi: Government Printer

Republic of Kenya. 2008. *Economic Survey.* Nairobi: Government Printer.

Rizzo, M. 2002. Being taken for a rise: privatisation of the Dar es Salaam transport system 1983–1998. *Journal of Modern African Studies*, 40 (1): 133–157.

Robinson, J. 2002. Global and world cities: a view from off the map. *International Journal of Urban and Regional Research* 26 (3): 531–54

Robinson, J. 2008. Developing ordinary cities: city visioning processes in Durban and Johannesburg. *Environment and Planning A*, 40 (1): 74–87.

Rodriguez-Pose, A. 2013. Do institutions matter for regional development? *Regional Studies*, 47 (7): 1034–1047.

Roy, A. 2009. The 21st-century metropolis: new geographies of theory. *Regional Studies*, 43 (6): 819–830.

Schabauer, H., Schikuta, E. and Weishäupl, T. 2005. *Solving very large travelling salesman problems by SOM parallelization on cluster architectures.* Vienna: University of Vienna.

Schalekamp, H. and Behrens, R. 2013. Engaging the paratransit sector in Cape Town on public transport reform: Progress, process and risks. *Research in Transportation Economics*, 39 (1): 185–190.

Schalekamp, H., Mfinanga, D., Wilkinson, P. and Behrens, R. 2012. *An international review of paratransit regulation and integration experiences: Lessons for public transport system rationalisation and improvement in African cities.* Cape Town: African Centre of Excellence for Studies in Public Transport and Non-motorised Transport.

Schweitzer, L. and Valenzuela Jr., A. 2004. Environmental injustice and transportation: the claims and the evidence. *Journal of Transportation Literature*, 18 (4): 383–398.

Shorter, A. and Onyancha, E. 1997. *Secularism in Africa: A Case Study-Nairobi City*, Nairobi: Paulines Publications Africa.

Schumpeter, J.A. 2008. *Capitalism, Socialism and Democracy.* New York: Harperperennial Modern Thought.

Schumacher, E.F. 1993. *Small is beautiful.* London: Vintage.

Senge, P.M. 1990. *The Fifth Discipline: The Art and Practice of the Learning Organisation.* New York: Doubleday & Company, Inc.

Shane, S. 2003. *A General Theory of Entrepreneurship: The Individual-Opportunity Nexus.* Cheltenham: Edward Elgar.

Stata, R. 1989. Organisational learning: The key to management innovation. *Sloan Management Review*, 30 (3): 63–74.

Stiglitz, J. 2002. *Globalization and its Discontents*. London: Penguin Books.

Soper, R. 1981. A survey of the irrigation systems of the Marakwet. In *Kerio Valley: Past, Present and Future*, 75–79. Edited by B.E. Kipkorir, R. Soper and J.S. Ssenyonga. Nairobi: Eleza Services Limited.

Sunday Nation, 23/3/1997, 'Outrage over City Lynching', pg. 1, col. 1, by Sunday Nation Team.

SWISS Commission for UNESCO. 2012. *World Heritage in Switzerland*. Berne: Swiss Commission for UNESCO.

The Constitution of Kenya 2010. Nairobi. International Institute for Legislative Affairs.

The Weekly Review. 1981. Death ride: matatus responsible for most road fatalities. *The Weekly Review*, 6 February, p. 11

Toffler, A. 1970. *Future Shock*. New York: Bantam Books.

Tuan, Y.F. 2011. *Space and Place: the Perspective of Experience*. Minneapolis: University of Minnesota Press.

Ullman, E. 1957. *American Commodity Flow*. Washington, D.C.: University of Washington Press.

Urry, J. 2007. *Mobilities*. Cambridge: Polity Press.

United Nations Development Programme. 2005. *Linking Industrialization with Human Development: Fourth Kenya Human Development Report*. Nairobi: United Nations Development Programme.

Unisa Centre for Corporate Citizenship, Barloworld Limited, Federal Ministry for Economic Cooperation and Development (Germany), Global Compact and GTZ (Gesellschaft für Technische Zusammenarbeit). 2007. *Africaleads*. Pretoria: University of South Africa Press.

van Vilet, E.D.S. and Kinney, P.L. 2007. Impacts of roadway emissions on urban particulate matter concentrations in sub-Saharan Africa: new evidence from Nairobi, Kenya. *Environmental Research Letters*, 2: 1–5.

Vasconcellos, E.A. 2001. *Urban Transport, Environment and Equity: The Case for Developing Countries*. London: Earthscan Publications.

Venkataraman, S. 2011. Entrepreneurship and entrepreneurial opportunity: made as well as found, in (Eds) R.K. Mitchell and R.N. Dino *In Search of Research Excellence: Exemplars in Entrepreneurship*. Cheltenham: Edward Elgar, 97–115.

Wacquant, L.J.D. 1992. Towards a social praxeology: the structure of Bourdieu's sociology. In *An Invitation to Reflexive Sociology*, 1–6. Edited by P. Bourdieu and L.J.D. Wacquant. Chicago: University of Chicago Press.

Wambururu Blog. 2014. The pro's and con's of investing in the matatu industry. *Wambururu's Blog: Matatus: Kenyan Mode of Public Transport Vehicles*, [Online]. Available at: http://wambururu.wordpress.com/2012/11/27/the-pros-and-cons-of-investing-in-the-matatu-industry/ [Accessed on 19 April 2014].

Wamue, G.N. 2001. Revisiting our indigenous shrines through Mungiki. *African Affairs*, 100 (400): 453–467.

wa Mungai, M. and Samper, D.A. 2006. No mercy, no remorse: Nairobi's matatu mode of travel and passengers' personal experience narratives. *Africa Today*, 52 (3): 51–81.

Wanzala, J. Cashless matatu payment system runs into opposition. (2014). Standard Digital, [Online]. Available at: https://www.standardmedia.co.ke/m/story.php?articleID=2000105373&story_title=Cashless-matatu-payment-system-runs-into-opposition [Accessed on 21 April 2014].

Watoro, K. 1999. Self-help group now a source of trade loans. *Daily Nation on the Web*, [Online]. Available at: http://allafrica.com/stories/199907130039.html. [Accessed on 21 April 2014].

Wawire, N.H., and Nafukho, F.M. 2010. Factors affecting the management of women groups micro, small and medium enterprises in Kakamega district, Kenya. *Journal of European Industrial Training*, 34 (2): 128–152.

White, H.P. and Senior, M.L. 1983. *Transport Geography*. London: Longman.

Whitelegg, J. 1987. A geography of road traffic accidents. *Transactions of the Institute of British Geographers*, 12: 161–176.

Whitelegg, J. 2013. *Quality of Life and Public Management: Redefining Development in the Local Environment*. London: Routledge.

Yunus, M. 1991. *The Grameen Bank: Experiences and Reflections*. Dhaka: Grameen Bank.

Yunus, M. 2007. *Creating a World without Poverty: Social Business and the Future of Capitalism*. New York: Public Affairs.

Zohlnhöfer, R. 2009. How politics matter when policies change: Understanding policy change as a political problem. *Journal of Comparative Policy Analysis*, 11 (1): 97–115.

Index